P9-DJK-058

JAKE MACDONALD | FOREWORD BY RICK HANSEN

RICK HANSEN'S
MAN IN MOTION WORLD TOUR

30 YEARS LATER

A Celebration of Courage, Strength,
and the Power of Community

GREYSTONE BOOKS

Vancouver/Berkeley

Photo on p. ii: A few more than 500 kilometres remain
and the crew can almost smell the Pacific Ocean.

→ Rick facing a crowd at the BC border.

Greystone Books Ltd.
www.greystonebooks.com

Cataloguing data available from Library and Archives Canada
ISBN 978-1-77164-344-3 (cloth)
ISBN 978-1-77164-343-6 (epub)

Copy editing by Stephanie Fysh
Jacket and interior design by Naomi MacDougall
Map by Eric Leinberger
All photographs, including cover, courtesy of Rick Hansen Foundation,
with contributions from John and Joan Tennant, Harvey Glanville, Dave Doroghy,
Maureen Shaughnessy Kitts, Nancy Thompson, Tim Frick, and Bob Redford.
Photos on pp. i and 162 by John Sherlock; 114, 132, 133 (top), and 145 (top right) by
Veronica Milne; 130 (top) by Pat McGrath/*Ottawa Citizen*; and 136 (top) by Glenn Olsen.

Printed and bound in China on ancient-forest-friendly paper
by 1010 Printing International Ltd.

Every reasonable attempt has been made to trace the original source of the images in this
book. Information that will allow the publisher to rectify any credit is welcome.

We gratefully acknowledge the support of the Canada Council for the Arts, the British
Columbia Arts Council, the Province of British Columbia through the Book Publishing Tax
Credit, and the Government of Canada for our publishing activities.

Canadä

CONTENTS

Foreword 1

1 When the Beginning
Seemed Like the End 7

2 He's Not Heavy,
He's My Brother 13

3 Building a Dream Team 31

4 Let's Do It 43

5 Taking Care of Business 53

6 The Endless Road 63

7 Show Me the Money 87

8 You Deserve a
Break Today 101

9 The Home Stretch 121

10 The Legacy 149

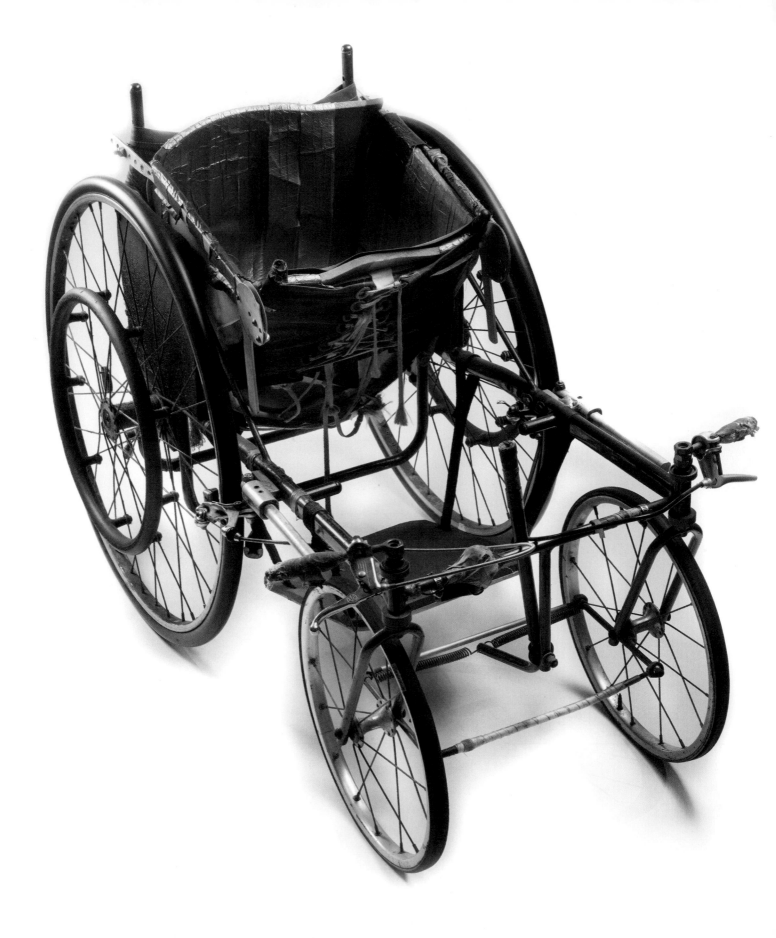

FOREWORD

—————

"Now this is not the end. It's not even the beginning of the end.
But it is, perhaps, the end of the beginning."
—WINSTON CHURCHILL

WHEN I SET OUT from Oakridge Centre in 1985, I was taking the first step towards my big dream. At the time, of course, I had no idea that the Man In Motion World Tour was the very beginning of a much longer journey. I just knew that I wanted to make a difference and that I was willing to take a risk to make it happen.

On April 3, 1985, I was confronted with my first pivot point. Less than two weeks into the Tour, my road crew and I had already run into skirmishes. I was plagued with injuries, and ahead loomed Siskiyou Summit, a high point on the road that stretches through a range of 2000-metre mountains between Oregon and California.

The Siskiyou mountain was a metaphor for the rest of my journey. It was the first real test of whether we were ready to take on this wild and impossible

1

dream. We were struggling so hard, and I knew that crossing that threshold would mean we were ready for what lay ahead. This was the end of the beginning for me.

I can't remember how the hours unfolded that day. Filled with tension and apprehension, we planned to climb the mountain in stages. All I could do was turn my focus inward for each three-kilometre stretch. I started with the first stroke and continued gripping the wheel, focused on how my body was responding to each push. When we finally summited, I broke down in tears.

Some of the best dreams in the world are defeated because we cave to the forces of failure. It's my hope that by reading this book, anyone who is nurturing a dream will find the courage to take that first step. It's never easy to sustain the journey. It takes resilience, grit, and tenacity.

Before the Tour, I had reconciled myself to the fact that there was a real chance I might have to abandon my dream, but I didn't want to have any regrets. How we conduct ourselves on a personal journey is as important as achieving it; it's a shallow victory if we lose our moral compass along the way.

The reality is that each day of a journey brings surprises, many of them tough. But each day also has beauty and magic. Sometimes you have to fight fiercely for those small victories: taking another stroke, crossing a threshold like the Siskiyou Summit, turning to a team member for a kind word, or returning a high five from someone along the road. Be present in those moments and celebrate them.

2

Thirty years have passed since the end of my Man In Motion World Tour, and I still reflect on that time with immense gratitude. During my darkest days, when I was overwhelmed by the enormity of the challenge and filled with fear, I know it was those closest to me who were my "difference makers." They challenged me to not give up hope and they supported me to continue looking forward.

This book is a tribute to all the staff, volunteers, road crew, board of directors, sponsors, community organizers, fundraisers, media, and people everywhere who supported the journey in ways big and small. Through hard work and determination—and through chance encounters, coincidences, and fated meetings—these people helped turn what seemed like an impossible dream to wheel around the world into a reality over 2 years, 2 months, and 2 days; across 34 countries; and along 40,072 kilometres.

The Tour became the greatest learning moment in my life, and that experience continues to shape my destiny and who I am as a human being. I wouldn't trade the life I lead now for the use of my legs. In being confronted with my accident, in taking on the Tour, and the journey since, I've learned that being open to the possibilities of a dream can open doors and pathways that I never imagined.

I couldn't have predicted that I would become founder and CEO of the Rick Hansen Foundation. The Tour marked the beginning of an ultramarathon of social change: it awakened the country to the potential of people with disabilities. Today, I've never been more optimistic about achieving my two original dreams of a world without barriers for people with disabilities and a cure for paralysis after spinal cord injury. Thirty years later I'm still chasing these dreams, but I'm amazed by what we've been able to accomplish together over that time.

All of us confront challenges in life, yet we can also identify with the Tour's message of hope and inspiration. My hope is that by reading this story, you'll be brought along on the journey and inspired to join me in finding your inner "difference maker." Together, we can shape the world we all want to be part of.

We don't need to wait for a crazy Canadian to wheel around the world, drawing attention to the values of accessibility, diversity, and inclusion, to create the country we want to live in. We all have the opportunity to dream big now and know that with the power of perseverance, everyone can make a difference. Dreams do come true.

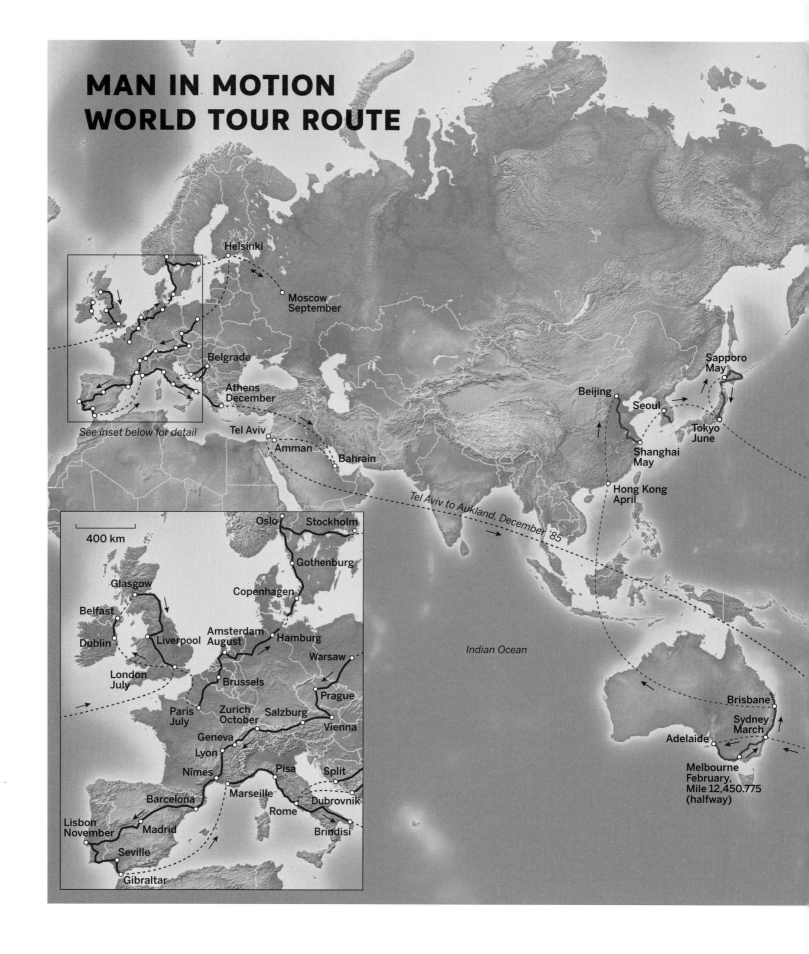

MAN IN MOTION WORLD TOUR ROUTE

Helsinki

Moscow
September

Belgrade

Athens
December

Tel Aviv

Amman

Bahrain

Beijing

Seoul

Sapporo
May

Tokyo
June

Shanghai
May

Hong Kong
April

See inset below for detail

Tel Aviv to Aukland, December '85

Indian Ocean

Brisbane

Sydney
March

Adelaide

Melbourne
February,
Mile 12,450.775
(halfway)

Inset

400 km

Oslo

Stockholm

Gothenburg

Glasgow

Copenhagen

Belfast

Dublin

Liverpool

Amsterdam
August

Hamburg

Warsaw

London
July

Brussels

Prague

Paris
July

Zurich
October

Salzburg

Vienna

Geneva

Lyon

Nîmes

Pisa

Split

Marseille

Rome

Dubrovnik

Barcelona

Lisbon
November

Madrid

Brindisi

Seville

Gibraltar

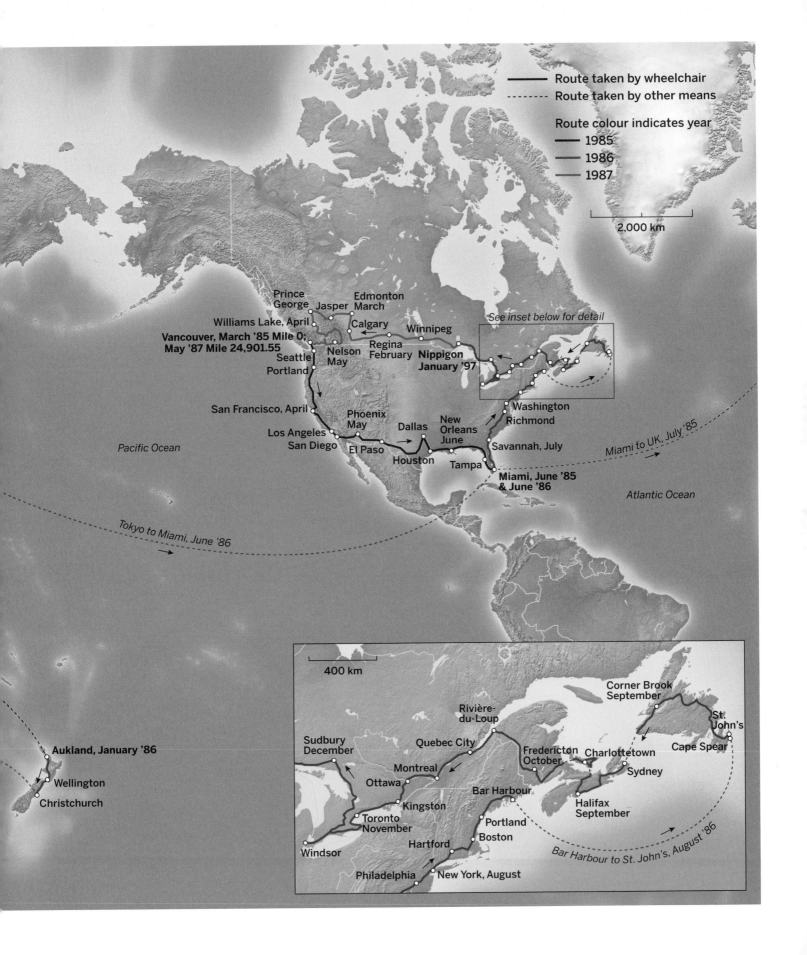

Route taken by wheelchair
Route taken by other means

Route colour indicates year
1985
1986
1987

2,000 km

Prince George
Jasper
Edmonton March
Calgary
Williams Lake, April
Vancouver, March '85 Mile 0;
May '87 Mile 24,901.55
Winnipeg
Seattle
Portland
Nelson May
Regina February
Nippigon January '97

See inset below for detail

Washington
Richmond

San Francisco, April
Phoenix May
Dallas
New Orleans June

Los Angeles
San Diego
El Paso
Houston
Tampa
Savannah, July

Miami to UK, July '85

Pacific Ocean

Miami, June '85 & June '86

Atlantic Ocean

Tokyo to Miami, June '86

Aukland, January '86

Wellington
Christchurch

400 km

Corner Brook September

St. John's

Sudbury December
Rivière-du-Loup
Quebec City
Fredericton October
Charlottetown
Cape Spear

Montreal
Sydney

Ottawa
Bar Harbour

Kingston
Halifax September

Toronto November
Portland
Boston

Windsor
Hartford

Philadelphia
New York, August

Bar Harbour to St. John's, August '86

WHEN THE BEGINNING SEEMED LIKE THE END

HIS NAME WAS RICK HANSEN, and he was a 27-year-old paraplegic. In the spring of 1985 he set out from Vancouver, British Columbia, in a wheelchair, determined to do what everyone said was impossible.

"When I first heard of his plan, I told him he was crazy," says advertising executive and broadcaster Fin Anthony. "I told him the most helpful thing I could do for him was to call in two doctors and get him committed."

Rick's dream was to push his wheelchair around the world—to spend 18 months wheeling through 34 countries. The weather would range from unpleasant to dangerous. The timeline would mean wheeling more than two full marathons every wheeling day. The chances of a serious medical breakdown or fatal accident were significant, and if he survived the 40,000-kilometre trek, he would come home without a nickel to show for it. Worst of all, he was abandoning a woman who was becoming the love of his life.

Why would anyone want to do this?

AS A TEENAGER in a wheelchair, and as a young man at university, Rick Hansen was the constant target of awkward glances, and he wondered how he could help create a more positive image of people with disabilities. What if he got in his wheelchair and pushed it around the world, demonstrating the potential of people with disabilities and showing that anything is possible if we allow ourselves to dream?

So on that spring day he spent preparing to embark on his dream, he burned with determination as he strapped himself into his chair. This dream wasn't just a personal challenge; it was a battle to change attitudes and raise awareness.

A crowd had gathered at the Oakridge Centre in South Vancouver to cheer him on, and as he powered his way out of the parking lot, the roar of applause was a blast of jet fuel. Like a fiery-eyed warrior of ancient Sparta, Rick was determined to come home with his shield, or upon it.

Rick was arguably one of the finest wheelchair athletes in the world, a veteran of countless marathons, but even the first day on the road proved to be much more difficult than he and his road crew had expected. His support vehicle got into an accident pulling out of the mall parking lot. His trainer and road manager, Tim Frick, wiped out on his bicycle just south of the city and narrowly escaped being run over by a car. A motorist following Rick and his convoy slowed down out of caution and was smashed from behind by another vehicle. Faulty map reading and confusion forced Rick to wheel two shifts of 48 kilometres, each one longer than a marathon. By the end of the first day he was a wreck.

Things kept getting worse. The March wind strengthened to 40 kilometres per hour and shot rain in his face. The van broke down. The hills were steeper than expected, and muscling the chair up the grades was punishing work. To make up for lost time, he sped down a hill and nearly crashed, narrowly escaping catastrophe. He was chilled, sore, confused. His left wrist started to fail him, then his right. The chair was uncomfortable; his arms and shoulders cramped from the torturous exertion of 9000 strokes per day. Long-distance wheeling had never felt this impossible before, and he began to fear that his hardened physique, battered and injured by so many years of competition, was finally beginning to break down.

Even worse was the pain in his heart. With every stroke of his arms, he worried about his girlfriend. He couldn't stop missing her. He had been lucky enough to meet the exact person he wanted to spend the rest of his life with, but he'd left her behind. Would she be waiting for him 18 months from now when he finished his reckless journey? Was that even reasonable?

He had only been on the road for a couple of days and already the crazy mission seemed doomed. Alone in his chair, pushing through the incessant wind and rain, he couldn't help wondering if he was a fool. Everyone had told him this project was impossible, but he had refused to believe them. Were they right? The most important element of any athletic challenge is staying positive, and his determination was weakening. By the end of the third day he felt deluded and beaten.

It was the shame and embarrassment that bothered him the most. He'd set out to show everyone what a guy in a wheelchair could do, and now he was failing the dream. He wondered how he could break it to his loyal road crew and his supporters back home that he was defeated. They would have a hard time believing it. Ever since breaking his back in that accident, he had never given up. He had always prided himself on analyzing the problems, finding a way past the obstacles.

As Rick sat there, trying to summon the nerve to tell everyone, it occurred to him that maybe, just maybe, there was a way to carry on.

But he needed to find a telephone.

> "He had only been on the road for a couple of days and already the crazy mission seemed doomed. Alone in his chair, pushing through the incessant wind and rain, he couldn't help wondering if he was a fool."

9

← Rick with schoolchildren in Delta, BC, the first stop of the Tour.

↓ Premier Bill Bennett (right) presenting Rick with a special Expo 86 licence plate for the motorhome.

← And they're off! Tim Frick (on bicycle), Rick's coach and the Tour's first road team manager, leads the way for Rick as he leaves the Oakridge Centre.

← Rick at the Peace Arch border crossing, before wheeling into Washington State on March 21, 1985.

↓ This motorhome donated by Vancouver businessman Jim Pattison became the Tour's rolling headquarters as Rick and the road crew crossed the United States.

HE'S NOT HEAVY, HE'S MY BROTHER

IN THE RURAL BACKWOODS of British Columbia where Rick grew up, a boy's strength and ability determined his status among his peers. Rick was an athlete, a natural leader, a stalwart adventurer.

Even as a toddler he ignored boundaries. His mother was forever out looking for him, asking, "Have you seen little Ricky?" Search parties would find him on the river with a stick and a string, trying to capture a salmon. One time he found a dead whopper and dragged it home; it was bigger than he was.

It was that same intrepid spirit that led Rick to urge friends to join him on a camping and fishing trip to the remote coastal community of Bella Coola in 1973. He was just 15 years old, and his mother thought the plan was reckless, but Rick wasn't a kid to take no for an answer. On a hot summer's day, he and his buddies travelled 300 kilometres to the spectacular mountain valleys of the Atnarko and Bella Coola Rivers.

They camped out, caught fish, gazed in wonder at fresh grizzly bear tracks, and experienced the sort of grand, intense adventure that only teenagers on the verge of adulthood can appreciate.

13

On the way home, they hitched a ride in the bed of a pickup truck. Through the rear window, they could see the long-haired driver and his girlfriend. And then suddenly the truck hit some washboard gravel and began to drift. The truck slid out of control, hit the ditch, and rolled. Fishing rods, tool boxes, and teenage boys flew through the air. "Don, on the high side, was thrown free," Rick remembers. "But I got crushed."

He was knocked out for a minute, and when he awoke he was lying in the ditch, in incredible pain, unable to feel his legs. His young life was just beginning, and his back was broken.

In those days, paralysis meant a grim prognosis: your life was over. Rick was rushed to Vancouver, and for two months he was strapped to a Stryker frame, which held his torso immobile while allowing his body to be turned to prevent pressure sores. He spent his 16th birthday in hospital. Finally, after seven months in the hospital and rehab centre, he went home to Williams Lake, where he tried to accept the fact that he was going to spend the rest of his life in a wheelchair. "I'd grown up in a culture where manhood depended on your ability to be strong and self-reliant," he says. "When I got home I was deeply bruised emotionally, and I couldn't see any way out."

He was the only kid in a wheelchair in the entire community, and he didn't want to be seen as needing help. His little sister, Christine, remembers how strange it was to see her once vigorous brother in a wheelchair: "I was only 7 or 8 years old and I thought he would just overcome it like he overcame everything. Dad revamped the house, fixed up the basement, and put railings on the stairs, but the railings would come off and Rick would fall down the stairs. He was always falling, but he would just pull himself up."

He was a stubborn kid, a competitor, and he told everyone that he was going to walk again, all by himself, even if it meant stiffening his unresponsive legs with steel braces, settling his arms into crutches, and hauling himself around with the muscles he was building up with hours of merciless weight-lifting. He didn't mind the constant struggle. It gave him an outlet for his anger.

14

Christine says he insisted on walking to school on his crutches. "One time I was over at a friend's house, playing after school, and my friend went to the window and said, 'Oh, Mom, look outside! There's that poor boy again.' I looked out, and Rick was going by on his crutches, hobbling through the ice and snow on his way home from school, just like he always did.

"I was shocked at her tone of voice. Did she actually feel sorry for my big brother? How could anyone feel sorry for Rick? He was my hero! I said, 'That's not a poor boy! That's my brother!'"

One hot summer's day some friends invited Rick swimming. They offered to carry him down to the lake, but his pride forbade it. If he accepted their help, it would mean he was less than self-sufficient, and he would never surrender to that idea. As the others frolicked in the water, Rick remained in the truck, sweltering. "I was feeling pretty bitter and angry," he recalls. "I didn't want to be seen as a dependent, but I didn't want to miss out on the fun either. I felt trapped."

He thought he could no longer do the things he loved. Never play basketball again. Never play hockey. Never dance with a girl at the high school prom. Never walk through the crisp, cold, autumn woods with a thermos and a hunting rifle or throw his tackle box in the 4 × 4 to go fishing.

"I guess my dad and my brother, Brad, brought it to a crisis point," he acknowledges. "They told me we were going fishing at this spot on the Thompson River where we used to go. I thought, 'The Thompson River Canyon? They know I can't do that! It's a difficult hike even for an able-bodied person. Why are they even suggesting it?' But they said, 'Get ready, you're coming.'"

The three of them drove to the Thompson River, unloaded their gear, and made their way to a swinging bridge over the river. "I was on crutches," says Rick, "but we headed across the bridge anyway. I went inching my way along, looking down at the rushing water through the missing boards, and thinking to myself, 'Wow, I'm actually doing this!'"

> "He was the only kid in a wheelchair in the entire community, and he didn't want to be seen as needing help."

15

When they got to the other side, where a steep rocky bank led down to the river, Brad told Rick to climb onto his back. Together, they clambered down to the riverside, and Brad set him up on a ledge with a lunch kit and a fishing rod. "Then Brad and Dad just left me there," Rick remembers. "So I sat for a few hours by myself, catching these jack salmon, having a great time, and it was a real watershed experience for me. It made me think, 'If I can still go fishing, maybe there are other things I can do. All I have to do is swallow my pride and accept help.'"

Instead of seeing assistance as a surrender to weakness, he started thinking of it as a gesture of strength, love, and partnership. "I began to learn that cooperation is a good thing," he says. "It's what holds families together. It's the connective tissue of communities and societies. It makes us all stronger."

Meanwhile, high school teachers Harvey Glanville and Bob Redford were also encouraging him. "When Rick came home from hospital, we tried to help him as best we could," recalls Glanville. "But frankly, he didn't seem to want anyone's help. He was very determined to do things on his own. Bob got this idea that he would get Rick to help with coaching volleyball and some basketball, but I think that was very hard for Rick because he used to be a star player and now he was on the sidelines."

"Harvey and Bob Redford taught me a lot," says Rick. "They encouraged me to stay connected with the team, coaching, and to dream big. It was about forgetting your ego and joining in, contributing what you could. They were great mentors to me."

Another important mentor was Stan Stronge. A skilled athlete who broke his back at the age of 30, Stronge became a role model and friend to many younger people living with disability, including Rick Hansen. "I was on my crutches one day when this guy pulled up in a red convertible and called out to me," says Rick. "I was a little suspicious until I saw the wheelchair in the back seat and the decal for the BC Paraplegic Association on the windshield."

An avid wheelchair basketball team manager, Stronge talked Rick into trying his hand at competitive table tennis. Rick practised hard, won a gold

16

medal at the Northwest Games in Seattle, and then went on to play wheelchair basketball for Stronge's pride and joy—the Vancouver Cable Cars. "Stan was my hero," says Rick. "He got me back into athletics and showed me what was possible. I don't know that I ever would have gotten back into competitive athletics if it wasn't for him."

Rick had always been a good student, and Redford urged him to apply to the physical education program at the University of British Columbia (UBC). "At the time, no person with a disability had ever been admitted to Phys Ed," says Rick, "but with Bob's encouragement I applied."

The university accepted him for a general program, but nobody in a wheelchair had ever tried to get into Phys Ed before and the faculty didn't think he could do it. The rejection was a big disappointment, and Rick assumed that it spelled the end of his dream of becoming a physical education teacher. But Redford wouldn't hear of it. He advised, "Go down there and enrol in the regular BA program and then apply again to Phys Ed, and keep applying. Don't take it as an obstacle. Take it as a challenge."

It was another important learning opportunity: Don't let people tell you what you can or cannot do. *Show* them. Rick left for UBC, determined to impress the gatekeepers and talk his way into Phys Ed.

Again, Stan Stronge proved to be a great ally. "He got me a part-time job," says Rick. "He helped me find subsidized housing and really encouraged me to stay involved in wheelchair sport. It took a number of people like Stan, Harvey, Bob, and of course my family to get me active again."

Sue Paish was at UBC, taking pre-law courses, and recalls the first time she saw Rick: "They had these Friday-night mixers where kids would drink and dance. I was standing in a group of people and some of the girls were making disapproving comments about 'some guy in a wheelchair' who was popping wheelies on the dance floor."

Everyone was standing around watching, and Sue sensed that the young man in the wheelchair was sending them a message—showing them that people in wheelchairs could have fun too. She was annoyed by the judgmental attitude around her and went out on the floor to join him. "I had never danced with a guy in a wheelchair," she remembers, "so it was kind of awkward, but I made it up as we went along and it got to be fun. I could feel everyone staring at us but I didn't care. I thought he was a different kind of guy, and I wanted to get to know him."

They soon became close friends, and along with Rick's girlfriend, Pat Leuke, formed an alliance that grew stronger as Rick progressed in his academic and athletic career.

Tim Frick was another UBC regular who noticed the guy in the wheelchair. "Rick was playing volleyball on a wheelchair team, and I came out to watch them play. They were just whacking the ball back and forth. Rick wanted me to coach them, but I told him, 'I don't know anything about wheelchairs, but I know about volleyball, and this won't do.'"

Tim recognized that Rick was working harder and was more committed than his teammates: "He was weight training and pushing himself pretty hard, so he and I began playing volleyball and working out together. We developed a theory that we could play well enough—just the two of us—that we could compete against an entire team of six able-bodied players." Soon they were challenging high school volleyball teams around the Greater Vancouver area. "We had a good serve that would get the other team off balance. We were skilled at feeding each other the ball, and strong teams would get a big surprise when they played against us.

"Rick wanted to demonstrate that a kid in a wheelchair could participate in school sports and have a fit lifestyle rather than spending phys ed class in the library. It was a way of educating people about the possibilities. And it really made an impression on those kids and their coaches. We played plenty of those exhibition games, two against six, and we never lost. Those volleyball teach-ins might have formed his later idea for the Man In Motion Tour."

Tim had a chance to move to the States and make good money as a trainer, but he decided to stay in Canada and work with Rick. "It was an easy decision

18

for me," he says. "An athlete like Rick is one in ten thousand. No matter what fiendish experiments I devised, I couldn't create a challenge tough enough to defeat him. Pretty early on I knew I had a character here who was destined for something great."

Wheelchair sport was still a relatively new discipline, and Tim and Rick were making up training exercises as they went along. One of the biggest problems was how to train in Vancouver's rain. "In the wintertime, it rains for months on end," says Tim. "So we built these rollers which were fastened to a stationary frame, and they were great. With Rick in his chair on the rollers, we could train in a gym and measure stroke rate, tension, heart rate, and other indicators you can't monitor as effectively when you're going down the road outside."

Whatever the sport—golf, hockey, or wheelchair racing—there's not much of a gap between losers and champions. "A winning package consists of a whole lot of little things," Tim explains. "Equipment, rest, attitude, diet, and so on. Rick was one of the first wheelchair racers to use the frictionless aerodynamic suits you see the cyclists wearing in the Tour de France. Our whole strategy was to try and gain half a percent wherever we could, on the theory that it would all add up."

The theory proved fruitful. Rick competed in the Vancouver Marathon and came third. He designed his own racing chair, built with lightweight aluminum and high-speed push rims. He won gold, silver, and bronze medals in the United Kingdom and beat some of his old rivals. Meanwhile, he trained ferociously on the rollers and built up his strength. The big shocker came at the Orange Bowl Marathon in Miami, where he not only beat the best wheelchair racers in the world but also crossed the finish line 14 minutes ahead of them.

During the early 1980s, he won 19 marathons around the world, including the Orange Bowl, where he once again trounced the competition two years in a row. In 1982, he challenged the Boston Marathon, uninvited, and knocked six minutes off the course record. In 1983, he shared the Lou Marsh Trophy with Wayne Gretzky as Canada's outstanding male athlete. He was on a roll, literally.

But he says the most valuable part of his experience as a Paralympian was not so much winning medals, but facing and overcoming other people's expectations. "You can imagine what it was like as a young man to be dealing with everyday rejection because of my perceived disability," he says. "Whether it was a cab driver who wouldn't pick me up or a waiter asking someone beside me what I would like to order, there were constant reminders of people's negative attitudes. My successes as an athlete were a way of educating them about the possibilities. That was the germ of the idea for the Man In Motion Tour."

Later in 1983, however, while training for the Boston Marathon with a new chair, Rick was speeding down a steep grade when he hit a bump and tumbled violently onto the asphalt. It was like a flashback to the truck rollover, only this time it was his arm that wouldn't move. Paramedics rushed him to the hospital, where he learned that his shoulder was dislocated. It was just hours before he was scheduled to fly to Boston to compete, but the doctors told him he wasn't going anywhere.

Dr. Jack Taunton, widely considered the founder of sports medicine in Canada, recalls, "I knew Rick from marathons we had raced in together. As his friend and medical advisor, I tried to get him the best treatment available." Dr. Taunton got Rick admitted to his old haunt—G.F. Strong Rehabilitation Centre—where he was assigned a highly regarded physiotherapist named Amanda Reid.

"I was just beginning to accept that I had a serious injury," says Rick, "and I was pretty bummed about it. But Amanda countered my fiery passion with a calm, conservative approach to rehabilitation that was just the right mix for me. Day after day, we worked on strength and flexibility. And thanks to her expertise, the shoulder started showing real improvement." The doctors cautioned that Rick's career as a competitive athlete was in question, and it would have been prudent for him to retire. But he didn't want to quit until he was back on top of his game.

He was, therefore, determined to repair his shoulder and get in shape for the biggest comeback of his athletic career—starting with the 1984 Paralympics at Stoke Mandeville, in the UK, and the Olympic Summer Games in Los Angeles. "I needed to qualify to get into the exhibition race at the LA Olympics," he says. "That was going to be the first time that a Paralympics event would be held at the regular Olympics. One of my burning ambitions was to get Paralympic events recognized as a legitimate Olympic sport, so I really wanted to qualify and make it to LA and be part of that event."

Amanda's innovative and incremental approach to rehab worked. Rick's shoulder improved, and after being discharged from G.F. Strong he went back to racing internationally—he won the 1500 metres in Stoke Mandeville by 3/100 of a second, won the punishing 42.2-kilometre marathon, and qualified for the Olympic exhibition race in Los Angeles by a fraction of a second.

As Rick wheeled out into the Olympic stadium in Los Angeles greeted by the applause of 80,000 sports fans, he felt that he had re-established himself as the world leader in wheelchair sport. But Rick wanted to take his athletic career to its biggest challenge yet: he wanted to race his wheelchair around the world.

"Sue sensed that the young man in the wheelchair was sending them a message—showing them that people in wheelchairs could have fun too."

21

← Rick received The Spring Horse from his parents for his first birthday and was soon galloping around the house. Even at that age, his eyes already showed his determination . . .

→ Always a keen fisherman, Rick shows off his catch with friends Randy Brink (left) and Don Alder (right) shortly before the accident in which he sustained a spinal cord injury and became a paraplegic.

↓ Williams Lake Junior Secondary had a number of active sports teams, including a strong basketball squad. Back row (left to right): Randy Brink, Tim Roberts, Rick Hansen, Gerry Hoyland, Ken Schmunk, Don Alder, Charles Wyse (coach). Front row (left to right): Mike Lee, Randy Shrumborski, Lawrence Morgan, Bill Blackwood, Terry Lindstrom.

↑ As his sister Christine recalls, "Rick was always wiping out on those crutches. But he'd pull himself up and keep going."

→ Rick with his mentor Stan Stronge, a formidable athlete who sustained a spinal cord injury at age 30 and went on to form a powerhouse wheelchair basketball team.

↑ The Vancouver Cable Cars wheelchair basketball team in 1979. Back row: coach Bill Lyons and Wayne Penny. Front row (left to right): Murray Brown, Dennis Cherenko, Peter Colistro, Stan Stronge, Eugene Reimer, George Boshko, Rick Hansen, Terry Fox, Charlie Quinn, Billy Inkster, Lenny Marriott, UBC gym, 1979.

→ Terry Fox (back) and Rick at the 17-Mile Labour Day Classic road race in Prince George in 1979.

← Rick (front) racing against Jim Knaub from the USA at the Pan Ams in 1982.

↓ Rick won nine gold medals in track at the Pan Ams, which was unprecedented at the time.

↖ In the 1970s and '80s, Rick travelled the world competing in wheelchair races. He won 19 international wheelchair marathons, earned 6 Paralympic medals, and set many new records as a wheelchair athlete.

← Rick (centre) playing for Canada against the US team in the finals of the Pan American Wheelchair Games in Halifax in 1982.

↑ Rick adjusting his marathon chair built by Tony Hoar.

← In 1983, Rick and hockey great Wayne Gretzky shared the Lou Marsh Trophy, which is awarded annually to the outstanding Canadian athlete of the year.

→ A Canadian sweep at the 1984 Paralympic Marathon Championship Open in Stoke Mandeville, UK. From left to right: Mel Fitzgerald (silver), Rick (gold), and André Viger (bronze).

3

← For wheelchair Olympic champion
Rick Hansen, the Man In Motion Tour
was the ultimate challenge.

BUILDING A DREAM TEAM

WHEN RICK ANNOUNCED THAT he was going to circle the world in a wheel-chair, there was no shortage of skeptics. But Tim Frick was a believer: "So far, Rick had conquered every challenge put in front of him. If it was possible to go around the world in a wheelchair, Rick was the guy to do it." Tim adds, "My main reaction was, when do we start?"

Just as Rick had learned to accept the help of his family, friends, and mentors back home, he was beginning to understand that this global tour could not be a solo effort. Nor should it be, for both practical and moral reasons. "I wanted it to be a group effort," says Rick. "By this point I had learned that we all need to surrender our egos and work with others if we are going to move to the next level and be really effective at bringing change to society."

Rick's old friend Terry Fox had become a global symbol of shared aspiration while attempting to run across Canada to raise money for cancer research. As Rick explains, "Terry's heroic journey inspired me and added a larger dimension. After Terry died, going around the world in a wheelchair wasn't just an athletic challenge anymore. It was a way of bringing people together for a common cause, liberating the potential of people with disabilities, removing

31

barriers, raising funds, and creating awareness." He began to see the global marathon as an educational campaign. And like any campaign, it would need a dedicated team.

One of the first people Rick approached for help was Bill McIntosh. An able-bodied marathon runner and the head of marketing for Nike Canada, McIntosh was a slightly older mentor to Rick and an astute advisor on business matters. He says, "One day in 1984 Rick and I went for lunch. The Expo 86 World's Fair was being planned for Vancouver, and the theme related to transportation and people in motion. I told Rick that a BC government ad agency had called me to see if I was interested in sponsoring someone to run around the world to promote Expo 86. Rick said, 'Why don't I do it?'

"We both agreed that this would be an amazing but very complicated project," adds McIntosh. "I said Nike would donate clothing, warm-up suits, and shoes for everyone on the team. But Rick also needed logistics, sponsorship, money, and people who believed in him. It was clear to both of us that he wouldn't be able to do it without a lot of substantial volunteer support, and the only way to get people on board was to put out feelers and recruit them one at a time."

Rick then called Marshal Smith, an outstanding wheelchair athlete who was the executive director of the BC Sports Hall of Fame and a vigorous promoter of wheelchair sports. "Marshal was an amazing guy," says Rick. "I knew him from different marathons. And at one point we spent a month in Hawaii together, training for the Orange Bowl Marathon in Miami. I came to really admire him, and he was the first on my list in terms of reaching out to the community."

Marshal soon made some calls to well-connected people such as politician Doug Mowat, prominent athlete Denny Veitch, and UBC athletic director Bob Hindmarch (who had supported Rick's eventual triumphant admission to the UBC Phys Ed program). Along with the colourful and influential Vancouver retailer Charles "Chunky" Woodward, physician Alexander (Sandy) Pinkerton, and lawyer John Tennant, they formed a board of directors.

Sue Paish, who was by then a young articling student, says Rick was so intent on making the tour a group effort that he didn't want to put his name on the project. "When I first talked to him about it, he wanted to call it 'World Wheel 86,'" she remembers. "But whether he liked it or not, it was becoming 'The Rick Hansen Man In Motion World Tour,' and of course along with that, his reputation was on the line. I guess he was beginning to realize that if he failed at this, that failure would be the main thing people associated with his name. So I feared for my old friend, especially when I saw how disorganized he seemed to be.

"I'm a very conservative and structured person, and Rick is pure passion and intention. He doesn't like to get bogged down in details. I was asking, 'What about insurance? What about permits? Police escorts?' He was saying, 'Why do we need insurance?' I said, 'Well, what if you cause an accident?' I was very focused on details, and he found all these questions kind of negative. He just wanted to get wheeling and do what he does best."

The new board members tended to side with Sue and other supporters who felt the tour needed to be delayed until enough money was raised and all the pieces were in place. Rick, drawing on the single-mindedness that had brought him such success in his athletic career, wanted to hit the road and let the home team sort out the details.

"The original departure window was set for early March," says home team manager Edie Ehlers. "But we had a serious sit-down meeting with the board only two months before launch day and faced the hard fact that we didn't have the essentials in place. We didn't have accommodation for Rick and the road crew. We didn't have gasoline for the escort vehicle. We hadn't figured out how to feed everyone. Nor had we devised a strategy for processing donations on the road. Worst of all, we had just $65,000 in the bank, maybe enough to run the tour for six or seven weeks."

Rick and the board had settled on an initial fundraising goal of $1 million, but raised it to $10 million even before the tour began. The target was put in place to measure their success: it would provide a tangible goal to spur their journey, and the donations would go into an endowment fund to support programs that raised awareness of spinal cord injury, improved the quality of life for people with disabilities, and advanced wheelchair sports and spinal cord research. These were noble ideals, but the tour wouldn't get off the ground unless they could find enough money to operate.

The board called a meeting with Rick and the road crew. It was a difficult and contentious showdown—the most serious crisis to date. Some members of the home team argued that the launch should be delayed until August, or even later. Rick and the road crew wanted to go right away. Several of the key supporters said they would resign if the launch date wasn't postponed. Edie says the final decision was left to Rick. As she explains, "One of the things we learned while putting this whole campaign together was the importance of a single, strong decision-maker. Any group that is considering doing something like this, I would caution them against making key decisions by committee. You have to have a captain, and in a crisis situation, our captain was Rick."

Rick says he understood their concerns. He hadn't completely recovered from his injury. The first leg of the tour would be through the United States, where the response to preliminary appeals of support had been weak. It was entirely possible they would run out of money while they were on the road. But he was even more concerned that one delay would lead to another, and they might never leave. He talked it over with his road partners. Don Alder (who had been with Rick in the truck on the tragic boyhood fishing trip that broke his back) had volunteered to serve on the road crew, and he said he was ready to go if Rick was. The second member of the road team, Rick's good-natured and energetic cousin Lee Gibson, said, "Hell, yes, let's make it happen!" Tim Frick was likewise itching to get started. Rick agreed with them.

Rick went back into the meeting and announced that, ready or not, the road team was leaving on March 21—as long as they had a support vehicle. Within days, Vancouver businessman Jim Pattison agreed to donate a motorhome, on the condition that the tour be called the Rick Hansen Man In Motion World Tour. "People relate to people," he said, "not slogans."

With transportation, an official name, and a departure date in place, the Man In Motion Tour needed to start generating publicity. But no one on the board of directors or on the management team had much experience working with the news media. They needed a savvy promotional person who could get news of the Tour into the media and keep it there. After all, the Tour's main purpose was to create awareness, and that wouldn't be possible without lots of free publicity across a wide variety of media channels.

As the rainy Vancouver winter wound down and March 21 loomed closer, veteran advertising man and broadcaster Finley Anthony (better known as "Fin," for his love of fishing) was identified as an excellent possibility. He and Chunky had become quite good friends because Fin had the advertising account for the Woodward's department stores. He recalls the day Chunky phoned: "I said, 'What's up, Cowboy?' and he told me he had met this young guy who wanted to go around the world in a wheelchair. 'We need your help, Fin. Come on over here, I want you to meet him.'"

Fin says his first impression of Rick was "this kid with an ear-to-ear grin" who couldn't wait to tell him about his plan for raising awareness about the abilities of people in wheelchairs. "He says to me, 'Mr. Woodward told me that you'd help me with the promotion, the newspaper articles, the television interviews, and such.' He just kept smiling and telling me about all the wonderful things that this world tour was going to do for public education.

"I asked him, 'What's your sign?' He said, 'Virgo.'

"I said, 'Cowboy, I suppose I'm stuck with this guy because Virgos are so stubborn that everyone around him is going to have to die and he's going to have to drop dead before he quits.'

"I told the kid: 'I can try and get you some publicity, but I can't guarantee it. Every guy and his dog in the city wants to get his name in the paper, and if

> **"Jim Pattison agreed to donate a motorhome, on the condition that the tour be called the Rick Hansen Man In Motion World Tour. 'People relate to people,' he said, 'not slogans.'"**

35

> **"There were hundreds of people in the crowd plus Rick's family, plus Terry Fox's parents, the local media, national television, and even the premier of BC."**

you think raising money is hard, wait until you try and get a reporter to listen to your story.'

"I guess I was pretty good at conveying Rick's story to the press, because we had a great turnout on launch day. There were hundreds of people in the crowd plus Rick's family, plus Terry Fox's parents, the local media, national television, and even the premier of BC.

"I was up on the stage with a microphone, doing my emcee thing, as Rick was getting ready to do his shotgun start. You know those overhead barriers in a parking lot that warn you if your vehicle is too high? Well, some genius on Rick's road crew lifted the barrier out of the way so that their overloaded motorhome could go under it. With great fanfare, I bellowed into the microphone, 'An-n-d they're off!!' And the motorhome zoomed off and crashed into the concrete overhang, tore the equipment from the roof, and scattered it all over the road. Of course, the crowd was shocked. It was not a great omen for the beginning of the Tour, but those boys didn't let it discourage them. They scrambled around, picking up the wreckage, and off they went!"

RICK HAD NOT been able to train sufficiently for the brutal physical demands of the road because of his injured shoulder and all the other demands on his time. On top of that, the weather turned foul, with strong, steady winds and hard rain. "It was so miserable," he says. "Three degrees. Sleet. Wind. I felt like I was getting hit with a baseball bat."

The effort of wheeling 8 to 10 hours a day into a mean headwind strained his arms and wrists, and by the second day on the road he was beginning to wonder if maybe they *had* left too soon. Maybe he should have babied his shoulder a little longer. Maybe they should have made sure all the funding was in place. The biggest missing piece in the whole messy picture was the piece of his heart he'd left back in Vancouver. By the third day, he was so broken in spirit and body that he knew he couldn't go on without help.

He dialled Amanda's number, and his heart lifted when he heard her voice. "His wrist was so stiff I could hear it crackling over the phone when he flexed it," she recalls. She was concerned, and like Rick, perhaps even relieved that his wrist injury was providing the emergency they both needed to force a reunion. "Do you want me to come down?" she asked.

Oh boy, do I ever. "When she said that, I was just flooded with relief," says Rick. "I didn't know what was going wrong with my body, but I knew I could face anything if she was beside me." She agreed to ask for her vacation time early from the rehabilitation centre and join him. Hanging up the phone, he felt a surge of renewed optimism. With his sweetheart joining him on the Tour, the dream team would be complete. With the aid of Amanda, maybe he could do this after all.

↗ Bill McIntosh (right) of Nike Canada presenting a cheque to Rick in 1985. McIntosh was a friend and mentor who helped inspire Rick to commit to the Man In Motion Tour, and Nike was one of the first corporate partners to support the Tour.

→ Expo 86, the World Exposition on Transportation and Communication, was held in Vancouver between May and October 1986. Rick was inspired by its theme, "World in Motion–World in Touch," and the organizers provided early support for the Man In Motion Tour.

← The Tour was guided by a strong board of directors that included, among others, Marshal Smith (left) and John Tennant, university pals, rugby teammates, and summertime loggers. In 1978, Marshal lost the use of his legs during surgery to correct damaged discs in his spine.

↓ Tim Frick (left) and Rick Hansen calibrating Rick's wheelchair for optimal performance before the Tour.

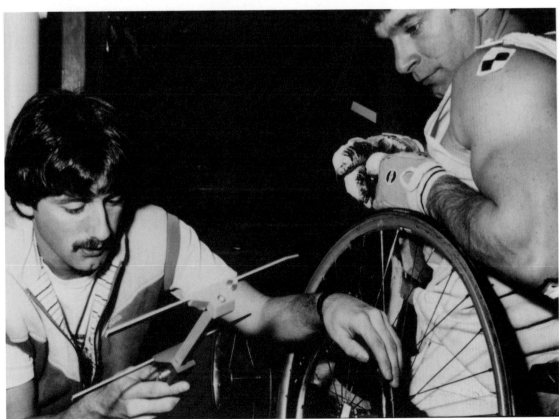

← Rick with Charles (Chunky) Woodward (left) of Woodward's department store and Herman Shad of the Sheraton Hotels, at the launch of the Tour at the Oakridge Centre on March 20, 1985.

↓ The send-off ceremony at the Oakridge Centre. From left to right: Rolly and Betty Fox, Premier Bill Bennett, Rick Hansen, Don Alder, Tim Frick, and Lee Gibson.

← Accompanying Rick on the Tour was his road crew. Don, Nancy, and Amanda were with him from start to finish; others came and went for shorter periods. Back row (left to right): Don Alder, Nancy Thompson, Amanda Reid, Mike Reid. Front row: Rick Hansen.

4

← Rick says, "I could never have launched the world tour if not for the love, support, and therapeutic skill of Amanda."

LET'S DO IT

RICK SAYS THE BUMP in the road that launched his wheelchair into the air, sent him flying down that hill in Vancouver, slammed him into the pavement, and dislocated his shoulder turned out to be the luckiest break of his life.

"Yes, I wrecked my shoulder and ruined my chances of winning my second Boston Marathon," he says. "But my physiotherapist turned out to be this stunning young woman named Amanda. She was not only highly skilled as a therapist, she was compassionate and beautiful, and every time we worked together, I couldn't wait to see her again." They worked on his shoulder, day after day, and their friendship grew stronger. "I thought about her constantly," he adds. "I knew we had to keep it casual, but I could feel our bond was becoming more than just professional."

There were roadblocks in the way of a relationship. Amanda was finalizing a divorce and was not ready to get involved in a romance. And she didn't feel that Rick was a good bet. "The wheelchair didn't bother me," she says. "One of the benefits of working with people with disabilities is that you learn to see the person rather than the disability. I could see that Rick was an extra-ordinary person, and there was definitely electricity between us. But he was

43

a handful. He was a cocky world-champion athlete, and I was a conservative health care worker. And anyway, he was going away for two years! I was wary of putting all my eggs in that basket."

But the growing bond between them was stronger than any misgivings, and by the time the Tour departure date was announced, they were a committed couple. It was a wonderful development in their lives, but terrible timing. They had no idea how they were going to sustain a long-distance relationship while he was on the road—or whether they were kidding themselves by thinking it was even possible.

For several weeks, Rick, Tim, Don, and Lee had been living together in Rick's crowded, messy apartment in order to acclimatize to being in close quarters. "That little apartment was just pandemonium with all those guys in it," recalls Amanda, "so Rick and I barely had a minute to ourselves."

The scene at Man In Motion headquarters was equally chaotic. The team had raised $90,000 in operating funds, including a grant from the Kaiser Foundation and $50,000 from the BC Lottery Corporation, plus free gasoline from Imperial Oil, motel accommodation, and other resources. But the stress of planning had been hard on everyone.

Amanda remembers, "On launch day I stood in the crowd with all the other well-wishers, assuming I would go off for lunch with my mom afterwards and have a good cry. But as Rick was leaving, he saw that I wasn't with the road crew, and he shouted at me with exasperation, 'Get in the motorhome!'" Weeks before, they'd discussed the idea that Amanda might ride along that first day, but they hadn't talked about it again and she'd assumed the plan had been shelved. But this was no time to argue. Amanda climbed aboard and they took off, following Rick as he pumped towards the international border.

The trip was just starting, and already they'd damaged the motorhome, smashed a wheelchair, embarrassed themselves on national TV, and snapped at each other. Amanda wasn't certain how this ill-advised relationship was going to end. After the first day of wheeling, she returned to Vancouver, unsure of when or even if she and Rick would be together again. She says, "I don't know what would have happened if Rick hadn't injured his wrist."

RICK MAY HAVE needed Amanda's emotional support as much as her therapeutic expertise, but when she joined the Tour she immediately focused on his physical problems. "Rick doesn't let pain stop him, and he thinks nothing of putting in a full day of hard exertion with a pain level of 7 or 8 out of 10. But he was risking permanent injury, and he just couldn't go on unless we made some fundamental changes."

Rick had severe tendonitis of the wrist and fingers and a pressure sore on his rear end from rubbing against a bolt that was sticking out of the seat of the wheelchair. "You can't take chances with pressure sores," says Amanda. "They can lead to dangerous infections. So I ordered a couple of days of rest with ultraviolet lamp treatment, which required him to just lie there and do nothing, which is exactly what he needed."

Before Amanda arrived, Don had been working on the chair, trying to find positions that would take the strain off Rick's joints. "But as soon as we devised a seating position that seemed to work, the pain would migrate to another part of my arms," says Rick. "I was packing my arms in ice after every wheeling session, getting regular massages from the crew, but I was a mess, both physically and emotionally."

Amanda was worried that the boys might feel she was crashing the party when she joined the Tour, but it turned out she made their group even stronger. Tim explains: "We had to share motel rooms, and sometimes we were banging around until after midnight and getting up again at four in the morning. So it was difficult to prepare without waking Rick. When Amanda came down and joined the Tour, it solved that problem. She roomed with him and we could work on the wheelchair until the wee hours in the other room without worrying about waking him up. When she showed up, you've never seen guys slapping high fives so enthusiastically in your life."

45

> **"...officers were helpful, sharing stories about their own friends and family with disabilities, escorting the team with flashing lights, and doing their best to get Rick safely through towns and busy areas."**

"Amanda is such a healer," says Rick. "Her presence had a calming effect on everyone. When I saw how positively she integrated with the team, I immediately started hoping that she might agree to join us for the whole Tour."

Amanda took over "all things Rick" so the others could tackle their own ever-changing list of tasks. The wheelchair was her first area of concern: it needed to be far more adjustable, with different-sized rims that could be quickly changed for different types of terrain. Steep grades called for large rims, which are slower but produce more mechanical advantage. On flat ground, smaller rims would allow the chair to go faster with less effort. "I had to work with Don on this," says Amanda, "and he was incredibly dedicated to getting the chairs running just right."

It was hard for them to know ahead of time what the road was going to look like the next day. Nowadays, programs that rely on satellite signals such as the Global Positioning System (GPS) have become so intrinsic to modern navigation that no bush pilot or cross-country hiker would dream of venturing into the wilderness without one. But these mapping technologies were unimaginable when Rick sat down with his road team before the Tour to plan their route around the world. As Rick learned all too painfully when he was slogging his way up the steep grades of the Oregon coast, a mountain road looks very different up close than as an undulating line on a map.

The lack of advance information on road topography was a serious problem, and its solution was Nancy Thompson. She had worked for the BC Wheelchair Sports Association before being drafted by Marion Lay, the Man In Motion Tour's headquarters planner and administrator, to help run the home office. "That 'couple of hours a week' quickly turned into a full-time job," says Nancy. "Rick was getting ready to leave, and there was frantic last-minute planning. We needed to organize public events, get telephone service,

46

contact embassies, coordinate with local police for escort arrangements, and do general coordinating on a whole range of fronts."

The proposed route covered a patchwork of jurisdictions. Nancy remembers, "One of the big challenges was figuring out who to call. You couldn't look up numbers on the Internet like you can today. We had to contact local police, sheriff's departments, state police, and highway patrols. We needed to get letters of permission from each to travel on the major roadways." The police sometimes argued that a wheelchair was like a pedestrian and was therefore not allowed on the highway. Nancy says, "We had to explain that Rick was much faster than a pedestrian, was on wheels, and needed to be on the road. It was a big educational process."

In most cases individual officers were helpful, sharing stories about their own friends and family with disabilities, escorting the team with flashing lights, and doing their best to get Rick safely through towns and busy areas. (As a gesture of appreciation, Rick began wearing a baseball cap with the crest of each local police service as he rolled through their jurisdiction.) But the Man In Motion team never did get permission to roll on Interstate 5 in California, so they were obliged to take side roads there.

Nancy recalls, "The original plan was for me to accompany Rick and the team the first day. But they were overwhelmed with tasks and asked me if I would stay with them on the road for another couple of days. That turned into three months." Her main role was advance reconnaissance. By then Don was constantly customizing the wheelchairs, altering the position of the seats and changing the rims to suit the terrain. Reconfiguring the wheelchairs needed to be done the night before, so Nancy would scout the road ahead and provide reports on the upcoming conditions.

"At first, I would take the Tour escort car and drive about 80 miles [130 km] ahead," she says. "I would make notes, saying things like, 'Okay, the shoulder is good, six feet [1.8 m] wide. There's a steep grade at Mile 22. At the top of the hill there's a McDonald's on the right.' And so on. Then I would write it up and rejoin the road team. So a lot of those roads I travelled twice."

To deal with the problem of ever-changing road conditions, Amanda came up with the idea of equipping Nancy with an altimeter and a tape recorder so that she could more effectively scout elevations, the percentage grade of the hills, curves, roadside rest areas, and anything else that might be helpful for the road team. "It got so that I was travelling well ahead of them," says Nancy. "That enabled me to do advance liaison work with community groups too. I would send my road reports back by courier."

She remembers that the crew learned to share bathrooms and shower facilities while on the road. "No one slept in the motorhome, because it was our shared kitchen and too full of stuff." Rick and Amanda stayed in one motel room, and Nancy, when she rejoined the crew at night, roomed with the boys in one of the others. "It was co-ed housing all the way. It was like rooming with your brothers. Wake-up call was 5:30 in the morning, so we were all running on minimal sleep."

Rick would stay in his room to eat a power breakfast of hot porridge, nuts, and fruit, prepared by Lee Gibson, who was quickly becoming the Tour cook. Everyone else would eat in the motorhome after it got underway. Nancy explains, "Once Rick was rolling in the morning, we were always busy driving, on the bike, planning events, doing the daily log, or out looking for phones and groceries. We took scheduled breaks during the day to give Rick a chance to eat, rest, change, and ice down his shoulders and arms, which bothered him constantly. Almost every day he was wheeling at a stage 7 pain level."

48

All the media's attention was focused on the stalwart young man powering his wheelchair through snow, sleet, and mountain passes—and rightly so. But no one knew better than the Man In Motion himself that in addition to his road crew, the Tour wouldn't have lasted more than a few days without the determined efforts of the uncelebrated team back home.

← Don Alder adjusting Rick's wheelchair.

↓ Amanda helping Rick to stretch and warm up before he sets out for his afternoon wheeling segment. Amanda typically spent 2 to 3 hours a day massaging, icing, and using ultrasound on Rick's muscles.

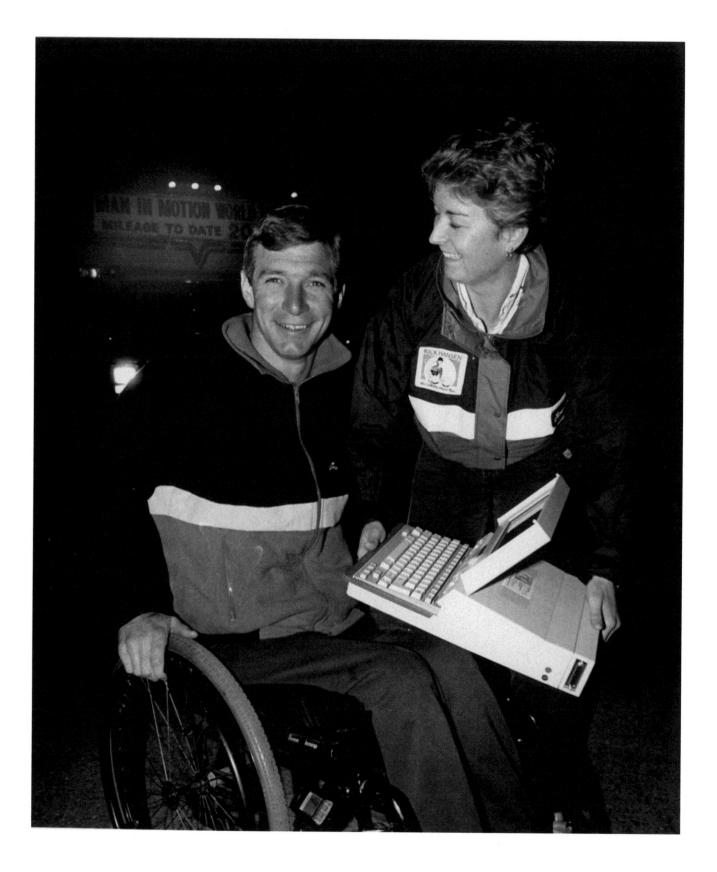

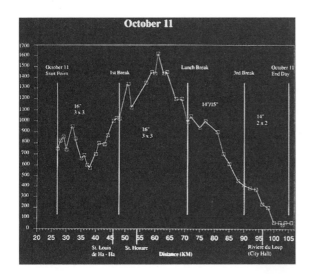

October 11

October 11 Start Point
1st Break
Lunch Break
3rd Break
October 11 End Day

16" 3 x 3
16" 3 x 3
14"/15"
14" 2 x 2

St. Louis de Ha - Ha
St. Honore
Riviere du Loup (City Hall)

Distance (KM)

↑ A sample of the daily elevation profile generated from the advance information and couriered to the road crew. It was used to plan the day's schedule, including break stops and estimated arrival times in towns.

← Nancy Thompson did advance reconnaissance of the route so the team could prepare Rick and his wheelchair for the upcoming terrain. Here, she and Rick review the details of the route on an IBM PC Convertible.

→ A computer mounted on Rick's wheelchair tracked every kilometre he covered around the world.

5

← A lot of the support work for the Tour took place in the home office in Vancouver, and it was invisible to the cheering crowds and the media. As Edie Ehler says, "Sometimes I think the volunteers got frustrated licking stamps, stuffing envelopes, and doing other mundane tasks while the road crew were having all the so-called adventures."

TAKING CARE OF BUSINESS

—————

AT FIRST, THERE WASN'T even an office. And there wouldn't have been an office, or even a Tour, if not for people like Marshal Smith and John Tennant.

Marshal and John had become friends as young students at UBC, playing rugby together, and working as loggers in the summertime. "Marshal was a great athlete," says John. "He was a handsome, friendly guy with tons of personality, and everyone loved him. When we went out on the town, Marshal would end up with all sorts of young ladies sitting next to him and I would be sitting there by myself."

They both sustained spinal disc injuries from playing rugby, and after a competitive tour of Japan, they realized they needed surgery. "I had the operation first," says John. "It went quite well, so I recommended my doctor to Marshal. As it turned out, I should have kept my advice to myself." Marshal came out of surgery paralyzed from the waist down. It was a terrible twist of fate for such a robust and active young man.

But, John says, "Nothing in the world could hold Marshal back. He moved on with his life, serving as the executive director of what was then called the BC Sports Hall of Fame and then, of course, he was recruited by Rick to join

53

> **"While Rick, Amanda, and the crew dealt with the uncertainties of everyday life on the road, conditions were just as chaotic for the home team."**

the board for the Man In Motion Tour. I would've done anything for Marshal, so when he called and asked for help, I immediately agreed."

John remembers how the Man In Motion board and the home office came together in the months before the Tour began: "I happened to be the corporate lawyer for Vancouver multimillionaire Chunky Woodward, who owned both the Woodward's department store chain and the Douglas Lake Ranch, one of the oldest and largest family-owned cattle spreads in North America. I got Chunky involved, and he became a key supporter of the whole effort. Rick was getting a lot of negative feedback from people who didn't think he could pull it off. But Chunky was very impressed by his energy and determination and believed in him."

John knew that the first thing the Man In Motion team needed was infrastructure and office space. But there was no money in the budget. "I called some of my friends at Cominco and got them to donate a year of free rent in a large beautiful office in downtown Vancouver. It was bare, but it was a great start."

Next, John and Chunky were convinced that fundraising needed to be a main goal of the Man In Motion Tour. "I think Rick felt a bit uneasy about the fundraising aspect because he wanted to keep everyone's motives pure," says John. "But I felt that in the end, he would be judged by how much money he raised. And in any case, they were going to need a substantial amount of financial support just to operate the Tour. The initial budget was $750,000, and I don't think anyone thought that was enough."

John and his wife, Joan, invited groups to their house to raise interest in the project. And he and Chunky organized what they called "wet lunches." "We would invite four or five people for lunch at Umberto's," he says, "and talk to the bartender ahead of time to specify that the martinis had to be triples. The lunches were partly about fundraising and partly about getting

54

people to throw their moral support behind the project." One person who responded was Jim Pattison, the legendary entrepreneur whose name is on billboards and car dealerships all over Vancouver. He offered the free use of a motorhome as an escort vehicle for the North American leg of the tour.

In addition to infrastructure and money, they also needed office staff. John talked to Marshal Smith about a possible candidate—Edie Ehlers, Marshal's assistant at the BC Sports Hall of Fame. John explains, "Edie could run the world. She is one of those rare people who can solve anything that comes at her and make it seem effortless. I knew she'd whip the operation into shape, if she was willing to take it on."

She wasn't.

As Edie explains, "I was employed by the BC Sports Hall of Fame and John was its unpaid volunteer chairman. He told me about this kid who was going to go around the world in a wheelchair. I thought, 'Sure he is.' I was very skeptical. Rick came into the office to meet with us, which didn't do much to convince me, because he had a black eye from wiping out in his wheelchair during a training run. I went home and whined to my husband, 'I don't want to do this!'

"I'm a fundraiser, and this tour was supposed to be all about awareness. Why did they need me? But the Tennants were behind it, and BC Wheelchair Sports were behind it, and Marshal Smith was behind it, so I was outnumbered, and they talked me into doing it. When I went over to the empty office it was even worse than I expected. There was no budget, no furniture, no phones, no anything.

"Meanwhile, the Tennants were all gung ho. And they know everybody. They were bringing in Chunky and Jim Pattison and various other influential people in Vancouver, who then started phoning other peers. The wheels started turning."

John learned of a company over in Campbell River that was going bankrupt and managed to get all their office furniture donated. Then IBM was influenced to loan a number of used computers, and Joan volunteered some of her acquaintances, and they got busy figuring out how to use floppy disks, daisy wheel printers, and all the computer machinery of the era.

"We still needed staff," says Edie. "So I found a program to top up the income of people who were on unemployment insurance if we trained them, and I looked for volunteers wherever I could. That's how Rico Bondi ended up working for us. I saw him in the elevator, chatted him up, and persuaded him to be our receptionist. He eventually ended up going out on the road with Rick in Europe and turned out to be irreplaceable as a member of the road crew."

The enthusiasm was there, but the money still wasn't. Disappointing news kept rolling in. Expo 86 announced that it had exceeded its operating budget and was cancelling financial support for the Tour. The best it could offer was the spare change from its fountain. John Tennant and Chunky Woodward did their best to twist the arms of Vancouver executives, but most donations were small ones from British Columbians who knew and believed in Rick.

"Even paring everything down to bare essentials, we couldn't get below a budget of $40,000 per month at home and on the road," says Edie. "And we didn't have anything close to that. We hired an expensive big-league fund-raiser who resigned after giving it a good effort, explaining that most of the reputable corporations he contacted simply didn't believe that anyone was capable of pulling this off. Even the more open-minded corporate donors were reluctant to commit, saying that they would consider getting involved later on if the Tour looked like a success."

And that was when Edie and the board members began to question whether the Tour was possible. "Rick had everything that you could possibly ask for in a leader," she says. "He had a strong body and tremendous strength of character. He had good people skills and charisma, and everyone on the team believed in him. But the unfortunate truth was, there wasn't anywhere near enough money to commit to a definite launch day."

But the Tour, of course, had gone ahead anyway. And while Rick, Amanda, and the crew dealt with the uncertainties of everyday life on the road, conditions were just as chaotic for the home team. "A lot of the work we did at the home office was invisible," says Edie. "That didn't bother me, but sometimes I think people got frustrated licking stamps, stuffing envelopes, and doing other mundane tasks while the road crew were having all the so-called adventures."

Some staff were volunteers, who couldn't be faulted for working at their own pace and showing up whenever the spirit moved them. Others were casual employees whose jobs were subsidized by unemployment insurance benefits, several employees were loaned to the project at no cost to the Tour, and still others were short-contract employees for a specific expertise in planning.

Muriel Honey was hired as the Tour's media representative. She had trained in broadcasting and television production at the British Columbia Institute of Technology and had spent many years writing radio commercials for an agency owned by Fin Anthony. "Fin was a great boss," she says, "and we remained friends even after I quit to have kids."

When Fin called roughly 12 years later, Muriel was working for Woodward's and raising a family at the same time. He said, "How are you doing, Muriel? I hear Chunky is making you work too hard. Why don't you come and work for Rick?" Muriel remembered having seen Rick Hansen take part in an exhibition wheelchair race many years earlier and thinking as he was interviewed afterwards, "Wow, what a guy!" But she never imagined she'd be working with him. "I already cleared it with the Cowboy, and we'll figure out a way to pay you," continued Fin. "It's only a couple of days a week, and Rick can really use someone like you."

She says Rick was wheeling his way down the west coast of the United States at that point, but he wasn't getting any attention. "They had no connections down there at all, and in any case, he was a Canadian, so nobody in the States cared what he was trying to do. So I became Rick's media person." Like Nancy, she says the "couple of days a week" soon became a full-time job (or "more than a full-time job if you counted the hours").

"We had a staff of twelve people by then, six on the road and six at the home office. There was no organizational structure, no policy, no nothing.

That was part of the beauty and part of the problem. I must have been fired at least three times, mainly because I felt I knew what was right for Rick and I wouldn't back down. Rick would phone the office, find out that I had been fired, and insist that I be rehired. It seems funny now, but it wasn't all that funny at the time."

She recalls the tension that often existed between the road team and the home team: "The guys on the road would get mad at us when arrangements got screwed up, and the home office staff would get resentful because the guys on the road didn't seem to understand how difficult it was to run the Tour at long distance. There was no cheap and reliable phone service like there is today. No Internet. No email. The fax machine had just been invented and wasn't in general use. Half the time we didn't even know where they were.

"Don Junker came in as a volunteer and made himself indispensable. He had come highly recommended by Chunky Woodward and John Tennant as a good problem solver and people person, and he ended up being the volunteer CEO of our office. He would get things all patched up between the road crew and the home team, pick up our spirits, and get us feeling good again. He was like our grandfather."

There was always excitement in the office when Rick did phone in. Edie says, "Everyone would gather around the telephone listening to the news, eager to tell him their problems. But Rick was very focused on his own job, covering those miles. And even though he took charge of major decisions, he didn't really want to get involved with figuring out the countless daily hassles we were dealing with at home. He expected us to solve those things on our own. His attitude was, 'Just do it.'" She says that turned out to be the right approach because it forced everyone to be creative. "The staff had to learn to do things that they didn't know they were capable of doing. In that way, we were learning, getting stronger and more adaptable, just as Rick and the crew were doing on the road."

Scheduling public appearances and media interviews involved a lot of guesswork because it was hard to know if Rick could make it on time.

58

"Nowadays cell phones would make it so much easier," says Muriel. At that time, "if we lined up an interview and Rick wasn't available, I would have to speak for him. I would have to put his thoughts into words, and I guess he was happy with the way I did it, because a trust built up between us. He was coping with bad weather, injured shoulders, steep mountain roads, flat tires, and all kinds of other difficulties, but he would never describe them as 'problems.' According to Rick, there is no such thing as a problem. There's only a challenge. So I definitely learned to avoid the P word."

One of the most important media connections turned out to be Vancouver disk jockey Terry David Mulligan, host of *Good Rockin' Tonite* and *MuchMusic West*, who was acquainted with celebrities ranging from Joni Mitchell to the founders of Greenpeace. Mulligan says he originally met Rick through Terry Fox, but they got in touch again when Rick phoned to ask if he could help arrange an introduction to the Expo 86 people. "Rick was inspired by Terry's example and had this idea that he wanted to wheel around the world," says Mulligan. "He thought it was a good tie-in with Expo, and I thought it was an inspiring idea. He was probably talking to other people for the same reason, so I can't claim to have been the reason he got connected to Expo, but I did whatever I could do to support him, because I thought he was a terrific guy."

After Rick left Vancouver, Mulligan followed his progress, wondering how he might help, and that's when he thought about his own friendship with the world-famous musician, songwriter, and producer David Foster. "As most people know, David Foster is Canadian and very proud of his roots," says Mulligan. "So I called David in LA and said, 'There's an incredible guy coming down your way. He's going around the world in a wheelchair and you have to meet him.'"

As it turned out, Foster and pop singer John Parr were working on the soundtrack for a movie and were having trouble coming up with the theme

"He was coping with bad weather, injured shoulders, steep mountain roads, flat tires, and all kinds of other difficulties, but he would never describe them as 'problems.'"

59

"Rick had everything that you could possibly ask for in a leader. He had a strong body and tremendous strength of character. He had good people skills and charisma, and everyone on the team believed in him."

song. Foster was captivated by Mulligan's description of Rick, and the image of the young man in a wheelchair struggling his way down the coast. "David was particularly intrigued by the phrase, 'Man In Motion,'" says Mulligan. "He kept asking me about it."

Foster is not hesitant to admit that he and Parr were more inspired by Rick and the Man In Motion Tour than by the young characters they were supposed to be celebrating in *St. Elmo's Fire*. Foster says, "Terry David Mulligan was urging me to write a song for Rick Hansen's tour but I didn't have time. But I was thinking about Rick pushing his way up through those hills and I came up with this little two-minute piece of music. Then I showed him [John Parr] a video of Rick, and the lyrics just spilled out of him. Listen to the lyrics: *You broke the boy in me, but you won't break the man… / Gonna be your man in motion / All I need is a pair of wheels…*"

Only weeks after the song came out, it was a number one hit on the *Billboard* charts. With its pounding rhythm and heart-stirring lyrics, "St. Elmo's Fire" went on to become one of the most powerful youth anthems in pop music history. "I still like to hear the song when it comes on the car radio," says Rick. "Although at one point on the Tour, in Portugal, it played for a week straight, and I have to admit, that got to be a bit much."

Mulligan's timely call to David Foster may have seemed like another stroke of luck. But as the great golfer Gary Player once quipped, "The harder I practise, the luckier I get." Out on the road, Rick and the team were working hard and making their own luck.

They were going to need it.

60

← The home team at the office in Vancouver with Marshal Smith (right), president of the Man In Motion Tour Society.

→ Rick with songwriter David Foster (left) and vocalist John Parr (right), the team behind "St. Elmo's Fire."

6

← Rick urged members of the home team to join them on the road so they could understand what it was like. Board chairperson Jim Watson took up the challenge. "It was brutal!" he says. "A bicycle is much more mechanically efficient than a wheelchair, but it was all I could do to keep up with Rick."

THE ENDLESS ROAD

IN SAN DIEGO, RICK and the road crew turned left and headed into the desert. Summer was approaching, and the ancient landscape was baking in the sun. They inched across southern California, Arizona, New Mexico.

By now the daily routine was well established—a wake-up call at 5 a.m., breakfast in the motel room, drive to the start point, wheel 8 miles (13 km), short break, wheel another 8 miles with another short break, wheel another 8 miles, then rest while Amanda worked on Rick's shoulders for two hours at the 24-mile (39 km) point. Same routine again into the afternoon, then finish with a final 23 miles (37 km)—the third gruelling marathon of the day—followed by media interviews and community meet and greets. The wheeling schedule varied with the terrain, the weather, rest days, and Rick's health, but on average they were covering 51 kilometres a day. (Over 792 days, that would add up to an incredible 15 million power strokes.)

Wherever they met people along the road, there was lots of cheering and support. But the American Southwest is one of the most sparsely settled regions of the country, with vast expanses of vacant desert, and most days the slow-moving convoy attracted little attention except from wheeling vultures. And as always, it was a challenge to get publicity.

63

They continued into Texas, a 1000-kilometre-wide expanse of oil derricks, pickup trucks, and cattle. Then on into Louisiana, with its French parishes, thundering traffic, roadside bayous, and steamy delta heat. Wheel on, wheel on. The highway was hot as a griddle under the merciless sun of Mississippi, Alabama, and Florida. "I just kept focusing on that specific wheeling section," says Rick. "In my mind I wasn't challenging the world; I was taking on a two-hour length of highway."

Nancy Thompson had solved some of their mapping problems, but as usual, new solutions led to brand new problems. At one point her tapes were stolen— all her road research covering three states. She says, "All that work probably ended up in a dumpster somewhere. Plus, I had only packed for a day or two on the road, so I had very little in the way of clothing, toiletries, shoes, and other travel necessities. It wasn't very pleasant wearing the same outfit for three months. But I was lucky enough to meet a lovely lady who sympathized with my plight and gave me a wonderful box of clothes."

Like the others on the Tour, she found herself making major sacrifices. In Vancouver, she had a job, an apartment, and a boyfriend, but after being away for several months, she realized that none of them would be waiting for her when she returned. "We gave up everything for the Tour," she says. "What made it tolerable was our shared belief in the mission and the constant reminder that Rick was having a tougher time than any of us."

The initial goal was to wheel 70 miles (113 km) per day for three days, take a day "off" for promotion work, and finish the Tour in 18 months. But that pace proved impossible for several reasons: it was too hard on Rick's body, it was too difficult for the team, and it made it too difficult to organize community and media events. Eventually Amanda insisted on reducing the pace to 50 miles (80 km) per day. "The media, communications, and public events were crucial to the Tour," she says. "And we couldn't take the risk of injuring Rick's long-term health." The reduced pace meant arriving home in May, crossing Canada in the winter, and missing Expo 86.

Rick believed that the best way to understand what the Tour was about was to experience it firsthand. He invited everyone he met to join him on the road for a few hours, and he particularly urged members of the home team—office staff, board members, supporters—to put in some time on the road, both to get a better sense of what the road crew was doing and to strengthen the bond between the two groups. One of the people Rick coaxed into joining him was Jim Watson, the Vancouver-based president of the national Kinsmen Foundation. Jim had first got involved with the Tour when Patrick Reid, Amanda's father and a commissioner of Expo 86, invited him for lunch and asked if he would be interested in chairing the Man In Motion board. Jim said he would have to ask his boss. "I've already cleared it with him," Patrick replied.

"That didn't give me much choice," recalls Jim. "So I agreed, as long as Patrick acted as co-chair. I attended the first meeting and was surprised at the shaky state of the finances, and I seriously considered backing out. But there were some very solid people on the board—strong individuals like Chunky Woodward, Bob Hindmarch, Dr. Sandy Pinkerton, and lawyer Russ Anthony—and if it wasn't for them I wouldn't have stayed on. Without them, Rick wouldn't have been able to complete the Tour."

Jim joined the crew as they were wheeling through Florida. "Rick kept warning me how hard it was going to be," he says. "But I didn't get it. I thought, 'I'll cruise along beside him on a bicycle. What's so hard about that?'" But it was 43 degrees Celsius when he arrived: "It was brutal! Bicycling in that heat, I was gobbling salt pills and going through gallons of water. A bicycle is much more mechanically efficient than a wheelchair, but it was all I could do to keep up with Rick. I remember constantly talking to him as we wheeled along to take my mind off the pain."

What also stood out was meeting and greeting everyday people along the road. "At one point I saw this little ragged African American kid standing in the heat on the side of the road with a few coins in his hand. He was obviously very poor, but he gave us his last coins, and that really hit me in the heart. I was also very impressed by the retired telephone workers who greeted us along the way. The home office had sent out messages ahead of time that Rick's dad was a telephone worker in northern BC, and they were a tremendous help."

Jim says that his weeklong shift with the road team was an invaluable experience. "When I got back to Vancouver, I told everybody, 'You have no idea how lucky you are. No matter how hard we are working, I can guarantee you that Rick is working harder than anyone.'"

In late June, the road team left the blistering heat of Florida and departed for the United Kingdom. The plan was to wheel across Europe and the Middle East, then head for Australia, New Zealand, China, and Japan. After crossing those continents, they would return to Florida, wheel up the east coast, then go across Canada and arrive home in Vancouver in time for Expo 86. That was the grand plan, but as John Lennon pointed out, life is what happens while we're busy making other plans.

Inevitably, they ran into delays caused by weather, navigational errors, mechanical breakdowns, and sickness. On several occasions the motorhome caught fire. Crucial supplies were stolen. Rick, Amanda, and other members of the road crew were weak and nauseous throughout much of the UK. Not only did they have the flu, they eventually discovered that a faulty exhaust pipe in their beaten-up old motorhome was leaking into the cabin—a situation that gave everyone low-level carbon monoxide poisoning and might have had deadly consequences.

Throughout the summer the weather was cold, wet, and miserable, and the team continually struggled with the difficulty of getting the word out. Their slog through rainy Ireland had been discouraging. The Irish leg had generated a total of $20 in donations. Raising millions of dollars? They weren't even breaking even.

"We had a much warmer reception in the Netherlands," says Rick. "The Dutch people are so thankful to Canada and the thousands of Canadian soldiers who died liberating their country in World War II. For me, it was a very sad and moving experience to visit the war cemetery at Adegem, Belgium, and lay a wreath in honour of those young men." Rick also got a warm reception in Denmark, Poland, Portugal, Belgium, and Yugoslavia. There were moments of poignancy when it all seemed worthwhile. But in general the constant difficulty of publicizing the Tour was frustrating. "When people heard about the Tour, they were very supportive," says Muriel Honey. "But the challenge was to let them know what Rick was doing."

Sports columnist Jim Taylor spent time with the road team in Europe and says, "It was a brutal routine for everybody. Rick was giving his utmost every day, and he demanded impeccable behaviour from the road crew. The newspapers would have jumped on any whiff of scandal, and Rick enforced strict decorum. But I felt sympathy for these young guys. They had voluntarily put their lives on hold for two years, and they were lonely. Rick was doing okay because he had the kind and beautiful Amanda for emotional support, but the guys on the crew had to live like monks."

"I felt very strongly that we had to conduct ourselves like professionals," says Rick. "We all started off as friends. But at some point I realized that friendship couldn't override the goals of the Tour. We had to be disciplined and constantly strive for improvement. Someone had to be the captain, and that had to be me—which put a lot of strain on our friendships." Rick told the team that if they couldn't conduct themselves in a manner that was beyond reproach, he would bring in a professional road crew and run the Tour like a business. "I didn't like laying down the law," he says, "but I felt strongly that the Tour was an opportunity for all of us to become bigger versions of ourselves. And we could only do that by putting our own wants and needs secondary to the mission. I just had to emphasize that the mission was more important than any of us, me included."

Even with ongoing pep talks and avowals of commitment, sometimes their bodies couldn't take it. Amanda was trying to juggle too many tasks and was wearing herself ragged. Don Alder was working late, retreating into himself, shutting the rest of them out with headphones. Tim Frick was so exhausted he couldn't see straight. "When you get really tired, you become oversensitive to criticism," Tim says. "Rick wanted me to be strict with the crew, but I didn't see that as my job. I saw myself as Rick's friend and coach, not as the task-master to the other guys."

What concerned Tim most was his own exhaustion. "On my days off I would sometimes have to drive the route ahead and make the notes," he says. "And I was so tired by the time we got to Austria that I was nodding off while I was driving. It really scared me. I was worried that I was going to cause an accident." He tried taking extra rest days and other stopgap measures, but they didn't help. "Finally I realized that I was becoming a liability to the Tour and needed to take a break.

"Typical of Rick, he was more concerned about my health than anything, and after a sincere conversation, we agreed that it was best that I leave. It was a difficult decision for both of us. We had this incredible friendship, and we'd been through so much together. But I was on the verge of collapse, so he let me go with his blessing. Then I went to a hotel and pretty much slept for a week."

When they were planning the Tour, Rick believed that the team would begin it together and end it together. "I saw us as a band of brothers," he says. "We swore that nothing would ever come between us. But as the Tour began to change into something bigger and more important than any of us, I realized that we were just servants to a bigger ideal. People would come and go depending on their ability to serve that ideal, and eventually we all came to understand that. And ironically, putting our own needs secondary to the mission actually made it easier for us to persevere."

Mike Reid was a classic example. When his sister, Amanda, left on the Tour, Mike was finishing up a degree in Phys Ed at UBC and considering a range of career options. "I looked seriously at playing professional hockey or becoming a teacher," he says, "but what really intrigued me was starting my own business. While I was going to school, I made money working part-time as a bouncer at dances and big public events, and I really enjoyed the challenge of dealing with difficult situations in an effective and diplomatic way. Most of the guys I worked with were sizable guys with backgrounds in sports, and we all got along very well. Needless to say, there was good money in it too! So I decided to start my own private security company when I graduated.

"One day I was driving home from Whistler, and the whole concept of my business was taking shape in my head. I really wanted to tell my parents about it, so when my mother called and said she needed to talk to me about something, I said, 'Good, Mom, because I need to talk to you about something!'"

The Man In Motion Tour was in Australia and New Zealand by then, and thanks to primetime exposure on national TV, they had been getting good public turnouts at some of their events. But, as Mike explains, the road crew were having trouble with crowd control. "It's hard to keep track of Rick when he's in the middle of a crowd because he's sitting, and with a jostling crowd around him there was potential for an unsafe situation to develop. And when he was rolling down the highway, it was often the situation that some mother would innocently push her child out onto the road with a $5 bill in hand, not realizing how quickly Rick's wheelchair and the motorhome were approaching. So there were security concerns. Rick and Amanda knew I had crowd-control experience, and they were hoping that I would come and join the Tour for a while."

Mike thought it would be a lark, a chance to see the world before he buckled down and started his business. "But I no sooner arrived," he explains, "than Amanda blew her top, threw a bowl of salad in Rick's face, and told him where he could put his Tour. She stormed out of the motel room and Rick chased her, in his wheelchair. She was running off into the boonies and he was madly wheeling after her. She jumped the fence so he couldn't follow, and he was pleading with me to go after her. So there I was, newly arrived with my backpack, innocently looking forward to an adventurous road trip, and suddenly I was in the middle of the *Jerry Springer Show*."

Experienced diplomat and tough guy that he was, Mike hunted down his sister, had a good straight talk with her, then led her back to Rick and persuaded them to kiss and make up. Amanda remembers The Night of Tossed Salad as a turning point: "I believed in what we were doing, and that night I decided that no matter what happened with Rick and me, I would stick with the Tour until it was complete."

Mike says there were other crises farther along, but the difficulties only strengthened the bond among the members of the team. For example, he says, "I got to know Amanda a lot better. I don't think that would have happened if we had stayed in our comfortable niches back in Vancouver."

Although Mike had joined the Tour to see the world, mostly he saw one long stretch of pavement. "We were so focused on getting through every hour of the day that we didn't have much chance to appreciate the countries we were passing through. And when you're wheeling down a highway, everything starts to look the same. Sometimes I couldn't even remember what country we were in."

The adventure came when Tour members got lost or separated from the rest of the team. Mike remembers, "One day everyone decided we needed some comfort food. We had these eat-free-at-McDonald's cards, so Nancy and I went out on a mission to find some good old burgers and fries. We showed the cab driver the card with the Golden Arches and he nodded happily as if to say, 'Oh yes, McDonald's!' So off we went driving through this monstrous city of Tokyo, and after half an hour we realized the cab driver didn't have a clue what a McDonald's was. Or maybe he was lost too. So we got out of the taxi and wandered around, trying to remember the name of the place where we were staying."

Neither of them spoke Japanese, and nobody they met spoke English. Finally, Mike did what any lost son would do: he phoned his mother. "I told Mom we were lost in Tokyo. She called Muriel Honey at the office, and Muriel figured out where we were staying. So four hours after we went out to get hamburgers, we returned to the hotel with nothing!"

He says every adventure and misadventure just made them more resilient. "My time on the road with the Man In Motion Tour was the major transformative experience of my young life," he says. "It strengthened my values. I had to make decisions that changed my life." One of those decisions was made in northern Japan.

"Traffic is horrendous in the southern part of the country," says Mike, "so they directed us up north to Hokkaido, where there are fewer people and less chance we'd get run over by a truck. But the weather up there was miserable—wet and cold. One night we went to this athletic facility and played badminton, and Rick injured his wrist."

It was early summer back in Vancouver. More than a year had passed since Rick and the road crew had left the Oakridge Centre, but they were still only a little more than halfway through their journey. "I was due for one week's vacation," Mike says. He was homesick for his friends, his family, and the beaches and mountains in Vancouver. "And I was really looking forward to seeing Expo 86. I hadn't told Rick and Amanda, but I was thinking that when I got home I wouldn't come back."

He was driving the motorhome that morning, sitting disconsolately behind the wheel with a coffee in his hand and the heater purring, and Rick was wheeling slowly ahead of him. Mike remembers watching Rick struggle with the blowing rain and the bitter headwind: "Rick's wrist was so swollen that he couldn't use it at all. He was pushing forward one-handed, dragging his injured wrist against the wheel to keep the chair going straight."

As Mike observed Rick through the clapping windshield wipers, one part of his mind was feeling guilty about leaving the Tour. Another part was missing all the fun back in Vancouver. "I had to make a choice. And I decided, no. I can't leave this guy."

Mike stayed with the Tour. Would he take on an arduous and idealistic assignment like the Man In Motion Tour again? "Not a chance," he says, laughing. "It was definitely the toughest thing I've ever done. But at the same time, I think everybody involved with the Man In Motion Tour became a better person because of it."

← The road crew in Arizona. Left to right: Tim Frick, Lee Gibson, Don Alder, Rick Hansen, and Amanda Reid.

↓ A wheelchair overhaul during an afternoon rest stop in Texas.

← Rick passed the 5000-mile mark in England. In London, he wheeled past Buckingham Palace and the Houses of Parliament.

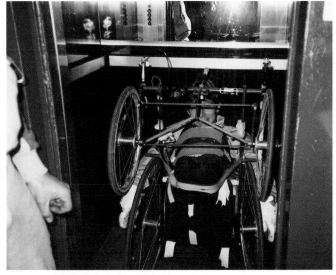

↑ One of the Tour's goals was to raise awareness of the barriers facing people with disabilities. Here's Rick in an elevator in France, hoping he doesn't get stuck between floors.

← Rick and Amanda met in 1984 when Rick injured his shoulder while training for the Boston Marathon and Amanda was the physiotherapist assigned to treat him. Amanda joined the Tour as a physiotherapist, but, like all the road crew, took on many roles. Rick and Amanda married in October 1987.

↑ Flat tires were inevitable, and Rick had 126 of them over the course of the Tour. The road crew got pretty quick at repairing flats and worn-out wheels on the fly, as Lee Gibson is doing here in France.

← Rick got to visit many of the world's most famous places, including the Eiffel Tower in France and the Leaning Tower of Pisa in Italy.

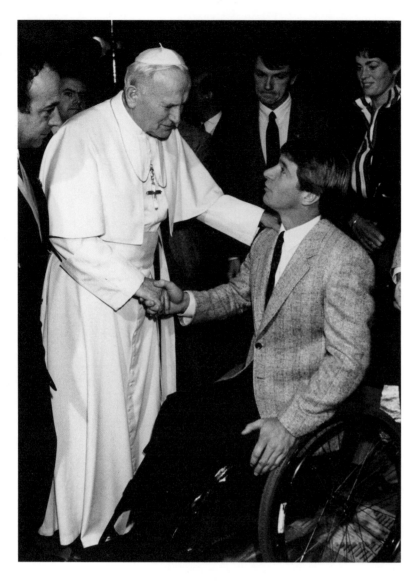

← Rick also met many dignitaries, including Pope John Paul II at the Vatican.

→ The Tour got a wonderful reception all over Poland, where people supported Rick with cheers and flowers wherever he went. Children were particularly drawn to him.

→ Rick wheeled about 8 hours a day with a member of the road crew riding a bike alongside him to be sure traffic didn't cut in too quickly. Amanda and Rick take a photo break in Yugoslavia.

↑ One of the memorable border crossings was this one over the King Hussein/Allenby Bridge from Jordan into the West Bank in Israel.

← Rick and Amanda also made a side trip to the Soviet Union, where Rick wheeled 5 kilometres, which included a visit to St. Basil's Cathedral in Moscow's Red Square.

→ Rick's Man In Motion Tour was inspired by his friendship with Terry Fox, who had begun a cross-Canada run to raise money and awareness for cancer research but died before he was able to complete it. Rick says his most homesick moment of the Tour came at this monument to Terry Fox in Jerusalem, Israel.

↑ On the road, Rick was often joined by local supporters, like these wheelchair athletes and cyclists in Bahrain.

← And he visited with others raising awareness of people with disabilities, including the Al Hussein Society in Jordan, which was founded by His Majesty King Hussein to provide rehabilitation and education programs and services for people with disabilities throughout the country. Left to right: David Malone, First Secretary, Canadian Embassy in Jordan; Rick Hansen; Colonel Yousef El Karmi, Secretary General of the Jordan Sports Federation for the Handicapped.

→ World events, of course, were taking place all around the Tour. Here Rick is wheeling past a mortar battery at a proving ground in Israel.

↑ Rick spent his first Christmas of the Tour in Auckland. Like many other travellers in New Zealand, Rick was stopped occasionally by flocks of local sheep crossing the road.

→ Connecting with kids to educate them about the potential of people with disabilities was an important part of the Tour. The crew distributed maps of Rick's journey so schoolkids could track his progress. Here he greets young fans in Geelong, Australia.

← By January 1986, when Rick and the crew reached Sydney, Australia, they had already travelled more than halfway around the world.

↓ On February 1, he crossed the 12,000-mile line at Kingston, Australia, between Adelaide and Melbourne, where the crew sprayed whipped cream. Ten days later in Melbourne, he reached the official halfway mark, 20,036 kilometres (12,451.49 miles), in his circumnavigation of the globe.

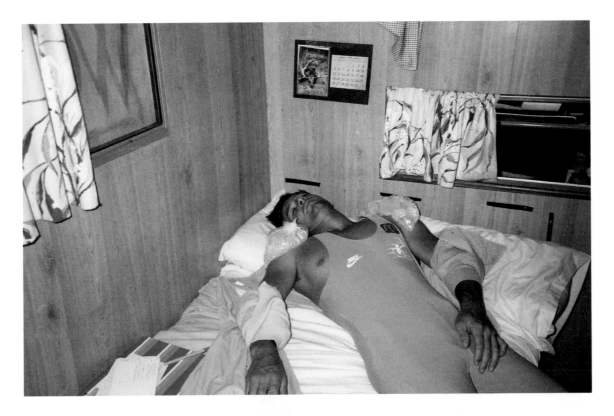

↑ Perhaps unsurprisingly, Rick was exhausted. By that time he'd been doing an average of 9,000 wheel strokes per day for nearly a full year.

← Rick wheeled an average of 8 to 10 kilometres per hour in the city or 13 to 15 kilometres per hour in the countryside. That's about half the comfortable cruising speed of a wallaby, which can hop at up to 70 kilometres per hour for short distances!

→ In Japan, Rick met with Princess Michiko (left) and Crown Prince Akihito (second from left), now the reigning Emperor and Empress of Japan.

7

SHOW ME THE MONEY

JOHN TENNANT, RUSS ANTHONY, Jim Watson, and other board members and key supporters of the Man In Motion Tour were big believers in the importance of fundraising.

"Rick was all about awareness rather than fundraising," says Jim. "That's partly because he's such a gentleman. He just doesn't like asking people for money. But his avoidance of fundraising was also about optics. He was very adamant that everybody understood that he wasn't profiting personally from the Tour, and that he would never take a penny of donated money. He thought it was best if he just stayed clear of the finances."

Jim, however, was convinced that the Tour would succeed or fail depending on how much money it raised. "The board agreed with me on that," he says. "It was going to be very hard to measure success in terms of public awareness. My attitude was, show me the money. So there was some tension there, with the two different visions of the Tour, and we had to work that out."

The Man In Motion Tour needed operating money—lots of money—to keep the road crew supplied with food, gas, and lodging; to run the home office; and to implement the goals of the Tour—that is, to raise public interest and support for the rights of people with disabilities and to fund medical research into a cure for spinal cord injury.

Rem Langan was the marketing director for the western Canadian division of McDonald's Restaurants when he got a telephone call from Doug Mowat, who was then a member of the BC legislature. "Doug Mowat helped us build Ronald McDonald House in Vancouver, a 13-bedroom house that accommodates seriously ill kids and their families," explains Langan. "He said he was helping this young guy who wanted to take his wheelchair around the world, and wondered if we would meet him. I was skeptical, of course, but I agreed to meet this crazy young guy, whoever he was."

Langan recalls the meeting at McDonald's headquarters in Burnaby: "He said, 'Hi, I'm Rick Hansen and I'm going to wheel around the world. Do you think you could help?'" Langan continues, "He had just kind of wheeled right up to my desk. But as he talked, and told me what he was planning to do, I was transfixed by those incredibly passionate, honest, direct eyes of his. It was obvious that he meant business. If it was possible to take a wheelchair around the world, I figured that he was the right guy to do it."

Langan asked Rick to hang on, and he walked down the hall to talk to his boss, Ron Marcoux. "I told him, 'I think you need to meet this guy.'" Marcoux met with Rick for 15 minutes, and Langan says his boss had the same reaction. "Ron said, 'Okay, kid, it's a crazy idea, but we're going to back you. For starters, we will provide you free meal passes to every McDonald's restaurant in the world. Get out there and show us what you can do. If you do well, we'll consider upping the ante.'"

Ron Marcoux told Langan to get on the phone, get McDonald's head office in eastern Canada involved, and bring in Palmer Jarvis, their advertising agency. "I called my marketing counterparts in Toronto and filled them in, describing Rick's energy, credibility, and of course those passionate eyes of his," says Langan. "They weren't convinced. They said, 'What's going on, Rem? Are you in love with this guy or what?'"

Langan and Marcoux decided they would go ahead anyway and try to convince head office later. They called Palmer Jarvis, one of the most respected agencies in Canada, and asked for an opinion from founders Frank Palmer and George Jarvis, who were good at tackling unusual projects. "We had a lot of admiration for Ron Marcoux," says Palmer. "He was a tough, iron-fisted western guy, and he didn't suffer fools. The fact that Rick had persuaded him to get behind this thing was definitely impressive.

"The guy who really got behind it was my partner, George Jarvis. McDonald's restaurants have a strong reputation as supporters of charitable endeavours. They're very community minded. Rick Hansen wanted to do public events, and McDonald's was always keen on getting people on site. It seemed like an ideal cross-promotion opportunity."

Jarvis and Palmer decided to put Dave Doroghy on the Man In Motion file. "I was surprised that they chose me for the job," says Doroghy. "I was young and very, very junior in the advertising business. So far my duties at Palmer Jarvis had included tasks like monitoring the costs associated with french-fry coupons, delivering posters to restaurants, and accompanying Ronald McDonald on school visits. I was just one level above the kid who filled the water cooler."

"Dave was a natural choice to handle the promotion campaign," explains Peter Fassbender, now a member of the Legislative Assembly in BC but then an ad exec with Palmer Jarvis. "He was young and energetic and had that entrepreneurial bent. The DNA of our agency was to take a crazy idea and make it work, and Dave seemed like the right man for the job."

Doroghy says he was excited about getting the assignment. "It seemed like a no-brainer of a partnership. Rick was the perfect worldwide ambassador for McDonald's. He was young, bright, articulate, and good looking. He was well respected and well known in Vancouver. Most of the countries he planned to visit had McDonald's restaurants, and his route generally followed the main highways and thoroughfares where the restaurants were located. The

89

partnership would give great exposure for his campaign and great exposure for McDonald's. I thought it was a McMarriage made in McHeaven."

Doroghy got busy helping Rick sew cloth patches with the bright red and yellow golden arches logo onto all of the track outfits that Nike had donated. He figured that the patch would show up well on TV and "garner the giant burger chain lots of exposure."

After Rick hit the road, Doroghy worked the phones, trying to plan McDonald's events. "I wanted to get McDonald's restaurants around the world fired up about Rick's tour. I developed promotional materials, brochures, video-tapes, and fundraising how-to manuals; translated them into different languages; and sent them to McDonald's restaurants along his route in the hope that the individual restaurant owners would plan fundraisers to coincide with Rick's visit."

To Doroghy's chagrin, "In the busy world of burger-frying, no one cared about some guy and his dream. Some of the restaurant owners were not only disinterested but actually hostile to the idea of a visit from Rick. I remember one McDonald's owner phoning me from the States, downright annoyed that we had sent Rick there. His restaurant was not wheelchair accessible, and he had no intention of spending the money to make it wheelchair accessible. A television crew had turned up to cover Rick's visit, and the owner was angry that we had embarrassed him and given his restaurant negative publicity."

As Rick wheeled through Europe, Australia, China, and Japan, Doroghy kept trying to plan fundraising events at restaurants along the route—and kept failing. "It was my big opportunity, and I was blowing it," he says. "The McMarriage made in McHeaven was turning into a McBust."

Warmer climates seemed to generate warmer hearts, and countries such as Greece, China, and Korea gave Rick a hero's welcome, even if they didn't generate a lot of donations. The reception in China was particularly zealous and helped to motivate Rick and inject some energy into the Tour. In the late 1960s, then prime minister Pierre Trudeau was determined to establish closer relations with China, which was just emerging from almost three

90

decades of dictatorial rule under Mao Zedong. Trudeau was an admirer of Chinese culture and visited the country a number of times. So when Deng Pufang, the son of Mao's successor, Chairman Deng Xiaoping, suffered a spinal injury, Trudeau arranged to have him flown to Ottawa for expert medical treatment. The young man's condition raised awareness of spinal injury in China and the favour was not forgotten. When the Man In Motion Tour arrived in China, the chairman's son had grown into a champion for people with disabilities, and Rick was welcomed by cheering crowds.

"Warmer climates seemed to generate warmer hearts, and countries such as Greece, China, and Korea gave Rick a hero's welcome."

While touring China, Rick fulfilled a lifelong dream of climbing the Great Wall, where the grades were so steep that his crew had to back him up and grab the wheelchair after each push to prevent it from rolling backwards. He attended endless state banquets and ate so much Chinese food he couldn't sleep at night. In some of the larger cities, he was surrounded by thousands of exuberant fans. In small rural villages, he was stared at by poor peasants who had never before seen a foreigner. Film crews and Canadian reporters followed him everywhere, recording his every move. "China was an unbelievable experience," says Rick. "It generated such optimism that we couldn't help being disappointed when we got back to the United States and there was so little response."

The lack of events in Florida and the rest of the southeastern coastal states translated into lacklustre fundraising, and once again, the Tour was at risk of running out of money. Edie Ehlers remembers that some funding they had hoped to get from outside of Canada hadn't materialized. "A lot of the larger corporations took a wait-and-see approach," she says. That left the coins from the Expo 86 fountain and many local fundraisers who were cheering Rick on.

Scientists weren't going to fund a cure for spinal cord injury with dimes and quarters from a fountain, but Edie says they weren't going to turn anything down. "We sent our volunteers to the fountain every day in gumboots

91

"While touring China, Rick fulfilled a lifelong dream of climbing the Great Wall, where the grades were so steep that his crew had to back him up and grab the wheelchair after each push to prevent it from rolling backwards."

to pick up wet coins, washers, and bent nails. They would bring the coins back, dry them on racks, run them through a counting machine, and roll them up. There was a designated room where we would tally up the coins and send them to the bank."

A TV crew came to the office one day to do an update on the Man In Motion campaign and decided to do a segment in the coin-counting room. "One of our volunteer ladies ducked behind the door while the TV crew was there," recalls Edie. "I asked her what she was doing, and she explained that she had been sentenced to a period of community service for petty theft. I thought, 'Hmm, maybe we should give her a job answering the phones or something!'

"From time to time we did have problems with fraudsters collecting funds under false pretences. There were cases of people putting on Rick Hansen badges and soliciting donations in pubs or out on the street," she says. As well, "Some news organizations were keen to 'get the dirt' on Rick, and they were looking for any evidence that he was exploiting the public. Rick is very strong in his upper body, and when he puts on leg braces and gets his crutches he can actually stand up straight. There were times when the media went crazy over that. At one point a film crew photographed him standing up, on his crutches, and the headlines said, 'He's not paraplegic! He can walk! He's a fraud!!'"

The Tour had been going for a year and a half by then. Yet "arriving back in the United States created the second and most serious crisis for me in the entire Tour," says Rick. "I was really dejected. It seemed like we were right back where we started."

"I told Amanda I had lost hope," he continues. "She sat down with me and validated my feelings, which was really important, then walked me through all the good things that had happened and were going to happen."

92

He counts that conversation with Amanda as his own fork in the road. "She restored my faith. If not for her, I would have quit, and none of this would have come to completion."

Amanda may have stoked his optimism, but the journey ahead *was* going to get harder before it improved. They were behind schedule and would be entering Canada just in time to meet the harsh Canadian winter, a situation they'd feared from the outset. As Rick puts it, "My personal crisis passed. But that didn't change the fact that we were coming to the toughest part of the Tour. We just needed to hold on to hope and keep the dream alive."

→ Rick met with the first son of China's former Paramount leader Deng Xiaoping, Deng Pufang. A paraplegic, Pufang has dedicated his life to improving the rights of people with disabilities. From left to right: Rick Hansen; Wan Li, Vice Premier of China; Deng Pufang; unknown.

↓ While touring through Asia, Amanda prepares Rick for the next wheeling session with a series of traditional stretches.

↑ The Tour received a police escort while crossing China, and local cyclists often rode alongside.

← In China, Rick was surrounded by crowds and received a hero's welcome wherever he went. Here he sets out for a day of wheeling with fellow athletes in Shanghai.

↑ By the time the Tour reached China, the media had started to take notice. Canadian filmmaker Michael French shot footage of Rick in Beijing and at the Great Wall and later made a documentary about this section of the Tour called *Heart of a Dragon*. Proceeds from sales of the video were donated to the Man In Motion Legacy Fund.

← In Tianjin, China, a record 800,000 people showed up to hear Rick speak!

↑ Built during the Ming Dynasty to defend Beijing from Mongolian invasions, the Badaling Great Wall is the best-preserved and most popular section of China's famous wall and has been visited by more than 300 foreign leaders and celebrities.

← Here's looking at you, kid. Rick shares a toast on the Great Wall of China.

→ A visit to the Dr. Sun-yat Sen Mausoleum in Nanjing, the final resting place of the founder of modern China. A team from the China Welfare Fund for the Handicapped, including several translators, travelled throughout the country with Rick and the road crew.

↓ In Korea as in China, Rick was greeted by influential politicians and thousands of cheering fans. That enthusiasm was a turning point for the Tour because there was a feeling that people around the world understood Rick's vision and were prepared to get behind it.

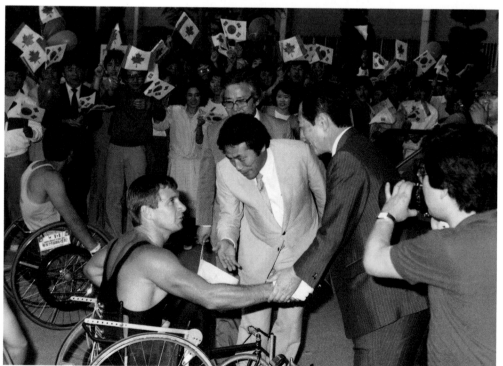

The Tour showed that extreme adversity can make people into better versions of themselves. As Rick points out, "If I hadn't broken my back I never would have circled the world, climbed the Great Wall, and met so many incredible people."

YOU DESERVE A BREAK TODAY

CHARITY, VOLUNTEERISM, TEAMWORK, and most of all determination drove the Man In Motion Tour. But luck probably also played a role. "Providence was a key factor," says Rick. "Whenever we really needed a lucky break, we got one."

And it was sheer luck that a Toronto businessman named George Cohon happened to have the television on one morning while knotting his tie and getting ready for work. Onscreen, NBC journalist Bryant Gumbel was interviewing a young man in a wheelchair. It was a segment that Cohon might have ignored—if not for the conspicuous cloth patch on the young man's shirt. That patch featured the McDonald's Golden Arches, and Cohon happened to be the founder of McDonald's Canada.

The young man was describing his incredible journey around the world: fighting his way through the Alps, meeting the pope, crossing the burning deserts of Australia, getting mobbed by tens of thousands of Chinese fans—all of it in a wheelchair. Gumbel asked him, "Why are you doing this? How is your body holding up? What kind of reception have you been getting in the

United States?" But as Cohon stood spellbound in front of the television set, he had only one burning question: Who is this guy?

He was perfect on camera: sparkly eyed, well spoken, and possessed of the sort of rare poise and honesty that go directly to people's hearts. This tour was exactly the kind of charitable project that Cohon wanted McDonald's Canada to be involved in, and Rick Hansen was Canadian!

Hearing that Rick was from Vancouver, Cohon called Ron Marcoux, Western Vice President of McDonald's, and asked, "Why didn't anyone tell me about this guy?" Marcoux insisted that for the past year, he and the Palmer Jarvis advertising agency had been doing everything they could do to tell people about Rick Hansen, and no one seemed interested.

"Well, that's going to change right now," said Cohon. "We have to get behind this kid." He says now, "I don't get that keen about just anybody, but I could see he was a true Canadian hero in the making. I called my public relations director, Maureen Kitts, and said, 'Mo, let's get the system behind this guy, and let's turn it on big time.'"

Cohon was—and still is—a legend in the international business world. A Chicago-born lawyer, he moved to Canada in the late 1960s with an agreement to license all the McDonald's restaurants in eastern Canada. Governing his empire with fearless style and a soft heart, he'd founded Ronald McDonald House Charities in Canada, opened the first McDonald's in Moscow (where the waiting lines were two hours long), and rallied the Toronto business community to save the venerable Santa Claus Parade.

McDonald's Canada was about to have a big convention in Vancouver. As Kitts recalls, "I met with George Cohon in his hospitality suite, along with some other marketing people, to discuss strategies for supporting the Man In Motion Tour. I think it's important that people understand there was no self-interest at work in George's enthusiasm for Rick's project. He wasn't excited about it because it was a marketing opportunity for McDonald's. George has always been energetically involved in charities. This was about supporting a worthwhile cause and nothing else."

"When George focuses on something," she says, "he goes after it like a great white shark." Cohon's enthusiasm for Rick's quest effectively turned up the heat under Palmer Jarvis, which in turned raised the temperature beneath the posterior of junior adman Dave Doroghy. "I had no excuses," says Doroghy. "Rick's campaign had raised very little in the way of donations. The trip across the United States had been a bust. I felt that we had let him down."

Doroghy wasn't surprised when the phone rang and it was his boss, George Jarvis, summoning him to a meeting. "George asked me what I was wearing," says Doroghy. "I thought it was an ominous question, and said I was wearing a jacket and necktie. My stomach tightened into a knot when he told me to meet him at an expensive restaurant, where we were going to be having lunch with the chairman of McDonald's, George Cohon."

It turned out he wasn't being fired. "They could have blamed the failure of the campaign on me," he says, "but they were prepared to consider that it had been difficult, if not impossible, for me to do advance promotion work long distance from Vancouver. They had decided to put someone on the road for the next year, travelling ahead of Rick, and that someone would be me. George Cohon told me that our goal, and my responsibility, was to raise a quarter-million dollars nationally for Rick. That was my pass or fail mark. A quarter-million dollars! That's when the knot got so tight I could barely breathe."

Doroghy didn't have time to consider the effect that a one-year absence would have on his friends, family, and personal life. Cohon and Jarvis just assumed that like everyone else, Doroghy would put the goals of the Tour first—and he did. He says, "This was such an important cause that I didn't hesitate to take it on. My only worry was that I would fail."

He flew nine hours across the country to St. John's, Newfoundland, checked into a hotel, and tried to figure out what to do next. "I got there several weeks before Rick arrived, but the pressure was already on. I didn't know one person in St. John's. All I had was a list of phone numbers of McDonald's restaurants across Canada—all 500 of them. The knot in my stomach eased off a bit when I did the math and realized we could hit our target if we raised $500 in each of them. But it tightened again when I remembered that the net take so far from all the McDonald's restaurants of the world had been zero. If I didn't pull this off, I would have wasted two years of my life, and I was pretty sure that my career in the ad business would be over."

The McDonald's restaurant empire is made up of small groups of restaurant franchisees called "co-ops." Each restaurant is privately owned, but the co-ops organize their local advertising campaigns and fund them collectively. They are free to pick and choose how they spend their advertising money and which promotions are going to work best for their region. "The person who owns the most restaurants is the most influential person and has the most votes," Doroghy explains. "I set out to find out who that guy was in St. John's, and pre-sell him on Rick Hansen." That man was named Keith King.

Doroghy says, "These McDonald's owners tend to be very busy guys. They are totally focused on their businesses, and although they might feel charitably towards an initiative like Rick's, charity is probably not at the top of their priority list." As Doroghy suspected, King was only vaguely aware of Rick Hansen, but he agreed to help. "I think he felt obligated to do something," says Doroghy. "He owned the first McDonald's that Rick would encounter as he was crossing Newfoundland, and he owned five of the nine restaurants in St. John's."

They discussed various concepts and settled on the idea of selling Rick Hansen buttons for the three weeks leading up to Rick's arrival. "In the McDonald's empire, majority rules, so the other four restaurants had to go along with our plan," says Doroghy. "I met with all of them, helped them design the Rick Hansen buttons, supervised the production of a radio commercial, and got some posters printed. We were ready for Rick a week before he arrived, but I still had two main concerns: Would anybody care that Rick Hansen had arrived back in Canada, and would the buttons sell?"

News travels fast in the McDonald's empire, and to Doroghy's great relief, the buttons sold, and sold well—6000 buttons for $1 each. "The buttons cost

50 cents each to produce," says Doroghy, "so we raised about $300 per store. To top it off, Keith King wrote us a personal cheque matching the amount we had raised in his five stores. The four other restaurant owners in St. John's quickly followed suit, and before we knew it, we had doubled our total, raising over $600 per store!"

With their legendary warmth, the Newfoundlanders threw a welcome-home party for Rick at Cape Spear, the rocky and wave-battered headland that is the most easterly point in Canada. There were fiddle players, speeches, and surprise appearances by notables such as Ethel Winger (the mayor of Williams Lake), Mel Fitzgerald (a pioneering wheelchair athlete and hero of Rick's), and George Cohon, who vowed to support Rick on his long journey home. For Rick, it was a gratifying return to Canada. "Ever since we left Vancouver we had been chasing rainbows," he says. "Chasing a pot of gold just over the next hill, and the next. We'd had so much bad luck that we felt we were due for some good luck. But we didn't want to get our hopes up."

The next day was Rick's birthday. He threaded his fingers into his leather gloves and launched himself forward, heading west on the highway leading back to Vancouver. "One of the amazing things that happened on that first day was the appearance of the girl with the buckets," says Rick. "She wheeled up on her bicycle with these two empty ice cream buckets attached to her back fender and a little homemade sign saying *Donations*. She had been watching the crowd and decided that we were missing donations because we were moving too quickly, so she volunteered to cruise along behind us. By the end of the day she had collected a garbage bag full of money!"

Media rep Muriel Honey had flown out from the home office in Vancouver, as had Jim Taylor, who was writing a book about the Tour, and it fell to them to count the cash in the garbage bag. "We went into my hotel room and dumped the money on the bed," Muriel recalls. "We were laughing like pirates because there was so much money, it was spilling all over the floor. But as we were counting it, we were touched by what all these coins and dollar bills represented."

105

Jim Taylor says that each donation had its own story. "All that day, as Rick had wheeled up and down these hilly roads and through these little villages of rural Newfoundland, poor, hardworking people had come out to stand along the road, to wave to Rick, give him their blessing, and hand him their donation. There were little kids on crutches with a quarter in their hand and old grannies with homemade cakes to celebrate Rick's birthday. It was really very touching."

The day's fundraising had been impressive. At a noon-hour birthday party in St. John's, Premier Brian Peckford had given Rick a cheque for $10,000. George Cohon had topped up the money collected at McDonald's restaurants in St. John's with a $4500 cheque of his own. The girl with the ice cream buckets had collected private donations amounting to $4700.90. "It was an incredible display of heartfelt faith by the Newfoundlanders," says Jim Taylor.

For Rick, it was a great welcome home. And it was, as he puts it, "a birthday I'll never forget."

THE CANADIAN LEG of the Tour had gotten off to a great start. The people of Newfoundland donated almost $100,000, and in honour of Rick's visit embarked on a vigorous campaign to build curb cuts from sidewalks to road level and install wheelchair ramps from raised entrances to ground level across the province.

The reception in New Brunswick, Nova Scotia, and Prince Edward Island was just as impressive, with enthusiastic crowds gathering along roadsides to greet the Man In Motion as he powered past. George Cohon had been so inspired by his experience in Newfoundland that he returned to wheel with Rick in PEI, which solidified their relationship and his faith that the Tour was making a difference.

Doroghy was counting up the donations with a smile. In Nova Scotia, 23 McDonald's restaurants raised an average of $910 each, well above the minimum goal set by his bosses. And again, the franchisees topped up the totals with their own donations. "I was learning to exploit the natural competitiveness of the franchisees," says Doroghy. "They enjoy outdoing each other in sales and were all very determined to beat whatever we had raised in the previous province. During the 12 days we wheeled through Nova Scotia, each day broke a record for the most dollars raised by a single McDonald's restaurant. And of course, the restaurant owners were also beginning to recognize the significance of the Tour and what Rick Hansen was trying to accomplish."

Mike Reid says, "I hadn't seen wild-eyed, enthusiastic crowds like this since we were in China. No matter how well intentioned, big crowds can be dangerous. And when I was doing my pre-event planning with the local police, I would have to say, 'Listen, guys, it's going to be crazier out there tomorrow than you think.'"

In Truro, Nova Scotia, he recalls, "I had a hard time convincing the officer in charge of our escort detail that he didn't have enough people assigned to the job. He more or less patted me on the back and said, 'Don't worry, sonny, we know what we're doing. We do this for a living.'" When 10,000 people mobbed Rick as he showed up to speak at a public assembly that afternoon, the police were helpless to keep order. "Thank goodness no one was trampled," says Mike.

"That individual officer apologized to me later, and called his colleagues in the next town to caution them that they needed to prepare for huge crowds. So the word went down the road ahead of us, and our police support for the rest of the Tour was wonderful, top-notch."

Rick and his road crew had been forewarned that it was going to be hard to drum up public interest and donations in *la belle province*. "I'd heard that the custom in Quebec is to give charity through the church," says Doroghy. "So I knew we were going to have trouble raising money for an Anglo marathoner, even one in a wheelchair." He was concerned that the wave of adulation that

"... through these little villages of rural Newfoundland, poor, hardworking people had come out to stand along the road, to wave to Rick, give him their blessing, and hand him their donation."

had propelled them through the Maritimes would flatten and die when they reached Quebec.

"But Rick, to his credit, conducted his media interviews in French. And although he was far from fluent, he made the effort, and that endeared him to the hearts of the Québécois. Second, he wheeled through Quebec with wheelchair athlete André Viger, and that really helped. The third thing he did right was to link the Tour with something that's as powerful in Quebec culture as the Catholic church—hockey."

In Quebec, the McDonald's account was managed by Cossette Inc., which also happened to handle advertising for the Montreal Canadiens. "The hockey gods must have been looking kindly on Rick Hansen," says Doroghy. "Because, as fate would have it, Rick would be wheeling through Montreal on Saturday, October 18, the same day that the Quebec Nordiques would play the Montreal Canadiens, a game that would be broadcast across the country. Our idea was to have Rick drop the puck at the Forum, in front of the whole nation, followed by a cheque presentation on behalf of all of the McDonald's in the province."

Doroghy and Cossette then persuaded the two teams to allow McDonald's to sell sports caps featuring their logos and the message "We're with You, Rick" in French. "Through Rick's association with the two teams, he would gain instant credibility," says Doroghy. "But we still had to sell the hats, which cost a buck to produce and would sell for $2 each. If I could convince the 125 restaurants in Quebec to order 800 hats each, the fundraising juggernaut we had created in the Maritimes would continue to gain momentum."

Well before Rick's arrival in Quebec, Doroghy invited himself to a meeting attended by all the McDonald's owners in the province. He'd prepared a 20-minute slide show and a "tear-jerking video" that showed Rick's journey to date, but the organizers told him he would have 5 minutes, if they had time for him at all. He says, "I gave it my best shot. But I could see they were totally uninterested in me and Rick. The entire meeting up until that point had been in French, so I didn't know how many people in the group could even understand me. After the most passionate pitch I could deliver, I asked each restaurant to pre-order 800 hats. They grudgingly ordered 100 each.

"McDonald's owners are very aware of promotional campaigns in neighbouring provinces," says Doroghy, "and as we headed into Ontario we needed to be building up steam, not losing it. After the meeting, the organizer told me that I was lucky because the owners had insisted at first they weren't going to buy *any* of the caps."

Once again, they got lucky. There were 14 McDonald's restaurants in Quebec City, and they were very influential. Seven of them were owned by Yves Simard, who was a passionate supporter of Rick Hansen and his cause. Simard met with Doroghy at the Château Frontenac in Quebec City and agreed to try to inject some energy into Quebec's lethargic response. Says Doroghy, "He said that he thought ordering only 100 caps per store was 'pathetic' and thought we should aim for 700.

"He said he would table a motion at the McDonald's meeting that day that each restaurant increase its order tenfold, to 1000 caps per store. He explained this would allow the owners wiggle room to negotiate down to 700, which was our actual goal. I thought, 'Wow, not only is this guy a compassionate businessman, he really knows how to make a deal!'"

Simard wasn't finished. He told Doroghy he would pressure the owners into ordering 700 hats per restaurant. Then he would say, "Dave, is there anything more we can do to support this wonderful cause?" That would be Doroghy's cue to mention that in the Maritimes most of the storeowners had also made personal contributions. At which point Simard would whip out his chequebook and fill out a personal cheque to the Man In Motion Tour. "The only trouble was, Yves had left his chequebook at home," says Doroghy. "But that didn't bother him. He said, 'Just give me yours and no one will know the difference!'"

At Simard's suggestion, he and Doroghy went into the meeting a few minutes apart so that no one would suspect they were in cahoots. The men assembled in the room with a stunning view of the river and the snowy citadel were an impressive lot. "They looked as if they had come out of an old black and white Humphrey Bogart movie," says Doroghy. "The room was full of thick cigar smoke. The men were all in their late 50s or early 60s, with craggy faces. They spoke to one another in French and barely acknowledged me when I entered the room."

Doroghy found a chair in the corner and listened while Yves Simard made a passionate speech in support of the Man In Motion Tour. "At the end of his speech he asked someone to table a motion that each restaurant would order 1000 hats," says Doroghy. "But the men only sat there in stony silence. He repeated his pitch in a sterner, more forceful voice, but once again, silence. Then he slowly stood up, thumped the table with his fist, and stared each one of his colleagues in the eye. He said, 'This guy Rick Hansen is out there in the freezing cold right now wheeling towards Quebec City. He is pouring his heart and soul into what he believes is right. He is wheeling 75 miles [120 km] each day to make a difference, and I won't allow him to wheel into Quebec City without the full support of each and every one of you!!' "

The room erupted into argument, recalls Doroghy: "They all yelled at each other for about five minutes until finally they agreed to order 700 hats per store. Then, with a wink, Simard asked me what else they could do to support this wonderful cause, and I recited my line about personal donations." With a dramatic flourish, Yves Simard drew his gold pen and started writing a cheque. No one spoke. They just watched in silence as he walked across the room, handed Doroghy the cheque, and said, "I don't know about you guys, but there is not enough that I can do for this great young man. I am donating a personal cheque for $5000."

Slowly, the seven other men around the table pulled out their own gold pens and filled out cheques for $1000 for each store they owned. "So thanks to Yves Simard," says Doroghy, "we secured $14,000 in personal pledges from the restaurant owners, plus orders of 700 hats per store, which all sold out. Combined with money donated from collection boxes at McDonald's counters and a car wash organized by Yves's restaurant, we raised over $35,000 in Quebec City, or about $2500 per store!"

On the night of Saturday, October 18, at the old Montreal Forum, Rick Hansen wheeled onto the ice to drop the puck to start the game between the Canadiens and the Nordiques. The standing ovation shook the rafters of the legendary old building, and Doroghy stood there clapping along with everyone else. "The applause seemed to go on forever," he says. "I had tears in my eyes, marvelling that this Québécois population everyone had warned us about was showing such love and admiration for this Anglophone kid from Vancouver."

After Rick wheeled out onto centre ice, McDonald's presented him with a cheque for all the funds raised in its restaurants across the province: $130,000. Rick says, "It was really an incredible show of support from the people of Quebec and McDonald's. It wouldn't have happened if George hadn't taken an interest." He dropped the puck, symbolically launching a fundraising wave that would gather momentum as it continued to roll through the last days in Quebec and into Ontario.

After more than a year and a half and 30,000 kilometres on the road, it looked like the Man In Motion's luck was finally turning for the better. "For me, the main purpose of the trip had always been to raise awareness," says Rick. "But I also knew that the success of the Tour was dependent on the amount of money we raised. That night at the Montreal Forum, I realized that maybe, just maybe, we had a chance of hitting both goals."

↑ When the Tour rolled into New York, Rick was interviewed on the *Today* show and visited with his friend and fellow Canadian Michael J. Fox. At the time, Fox was starring in the popular *Family Ties* TV series and in the *Back to the Future* films.

← Rick in Newfoundland with George Cohon, the President of McDonald's Canada. On the morning that Rick was a guest on the *Today* show in New York, Cohon happened to glance at his TV, became intrigued by Rick's message, and decided to throw the support of McDonald's behind the Tour. Cohon and the restaurants helped generate millions of dollars in private donations.

↖ After the McDonald's franchises in Newfoundland got behind the Tour, restaurants across the country followed with fundraisers and donation matching.

← McDonald's employees line the street to congratulate Rick and welcome him to town.

↙ Rick receiving a "We're with you Rick!" spatula from McDonald's during the Man In Motion World Tour on September 4, 1986.

← Hundreds of people lined the roadside out of St. John's, Newfoundland, to welcome Rick home, applaud him, and shout their best wishes.

→ Sonya Harvey, age 3, of Conception Bay, Newfoundland, presents Rick with a homemade birthday card she coloured with help from babysitter Mary Morgan. Rick celebrated his 28th and 29th birthdays on the road, but ultimately received thousands of pieces of memorabilia—from pins, plaques, and pennants to toys, T-shirts, and trophies.

MAN IN MOTION WORLD TOUR
MILEAGE TO DATE 17720
VANGUARD

↑ He began his cross-Canada tour in Cape Spear, Newfoundland, where pioneering wheelchair athlete Mel Fitzgerald joined him for the day.

→ Canadians welcomed Rick home with overwhelming encouragement and support.

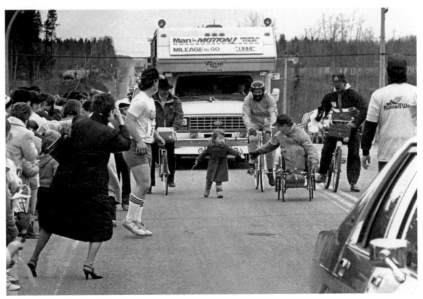

← Giving kids access to Rick along the road and at special events was a priority of the Tour. Whether speaking, signing autographs, or shaking hands with his young followers, Rick became a role model for many of them.

↓ Mike Reid examines a wheel after repair by chief mechanic Don Alder. Don was constantly adjusting the wheelchairs to suit the terrain. In Canada, an entire trailer was devoted to wheelchairs and wheelchair parts.

↑ Rick got a true Canadian homecoming. In less than two days, the people of Newfoundland raised over $97,000 for the Tour, money that would go towards research and rehabilitation.

← Rick rolls across the Angus L. Macdonald Bridge as he enters Halifax. The fundraising momentum established in Newfoundland carried through to Nova Scotia. The province raised $455,000 for the Tour.

→ Rick greeted the crowd at a massive community rally at Halifax City Hall.

↓ The Tour received a warm welcome from the young students at Belfast Consolidated School in Prince Edward Island.

9

← Something about the Man In Motion Tour fascinated kids the world over. Here Rick greets one of his young admirers.

THE HOME STRETCH

THE MOMENTUM WAS BUILDING as Rick crossed the country. After a victorious tour of Quebec, the Man In Motion rolled into Ottawa, where Prime Minister Brian Mulroney presented him with a cheque for $1 million.

"There's an amusing story to go with that cheque," says Muriel Honey. "After the prime minister dropped the cheque into the Kinsmen donation bucket, one of his aides retrieved it, not wanting to leave a big government cheque unguarded with all the spare change and crumpled $5 bills. Later, he gave the cheque to Jim Taylor and me, and when we strolled into the hotel we saw the Kinsmen feverishly searching through the bucket, looking for the cheque! They were much relieved when we waved it at them."

In Toronto, tens of thousands of people lined the streets to cheer Rick on and offer their support and donations. He was also the guest star of a black-tie fundraising banquet where David Foster and John Parr brought the crowd to their feet with a stirring rendition of "St. Elmo's Fire." Muriel says, "We spent 18 months begging people to pay attention. But by the time we hit Toronto, it went from no attention to too much attention. Reporters were driving me crazy, shoving notes under the door of my hotel room, calling me day and night. I don't stress out easily, but on my one day off in Toronto, I spent the day curled up on the bed in my hotel room crying because I was just plain overwhelmed."

Bill McIntosh had moved to Toronto by then, to become president of Nike Canada, and he and his wife invited Rick and Amanda to their home for dinner. "I think they really appreciated getting some peace and quiet for a few hours," he says. "Rick was feeling a bit uncomfortable with his new status as a celebrity. The news media love creating stars, but he had to keep reminding them that the Tour was not about him. It was about the issues."

Rick had to stay focused because he had months of dangerously cold weather ahead of him, and about 3000 kilometres of sparsely settled wilderness before he reached the middle of the country.

To prepare for the arduous conditions, he'd been equipped with a four-wheel-drive wheelchair designed by his old friends ace mechanics Pete Turnau and Jerry Smith. A winter technical team led by Brian Rose had created thermostatically regulated winter clothes with sensors to ensure that his legs did not suffer from frostbite. If the equipment could insulate him from the cold, it couldn't protect him from the sheer difficulty of what he was doing: pushing wheelchair rims coated with ice and snow forward through slush and wind that drained the energy from his body and made him more susceptible to the flu viruses that awaited him in every motel room and restaurant.

By the time Rick reached Wawa, Ontario, a town surrounded by vast wilderness and so dreaded by hitchhikers that it has inspired several comic songs, a flu bug had settled into his lungs and a bacterial infection had found a home in his bladder. Either of these was serious enough to rob an average able-bodied person of the energy required to get out of bed, let alone push a wheelchair for nine hours through bitter cold.

Rick couldn't help thinking about his old pal Terry Fox, whose cancer had returned when he'd tried to fight his way through this very part of the country.

It seemed too cruel to think that both of them might be defeated on the final home stretch through Canada. But Rick's body was faltering, and all he could do was pray for the strength to carry on.

He rested in bed, fighting off the infections, and celebrated Christmas with a turkey dinner with Amanda and the rest of the road crew in their Wawa motel. By New Year's Day they were back on the road, and this time luck seemed to be with them—they were blessed with atypically mild sunny weather and dry highways.

Near Thunder Bay, Rick paid homage to Terry Fox at the monument erected in his honour, at the very spot on the highway where cancer had ended the Marathon of Hope. "The word had gotten out that I'd arrived in town," says Rick, "and a crowd of reporters and spectators showed up with cameras. We had asked for publicity and we were getting publicity, but after travelling all those miles I had really looked forward to some quiet time with my old friend. It wasn't to be. I tried not to lose control of my emotions in front of all those cameras, sent a message to Terry, and got back on the road."

THE BOREAL FOREST is an immense wilderness of lakes, rocky outcrops, and evergreen forest covering about half of Canada. Just past the border between Ontario and Manitoba, the Trans-Canada Highway descends a gentle staircase of sandy ridges. The sandy slopes are the remnants of ancient beaches, and when Rick rolled down the final beach onto the Manitoba farmlands, he was entering the ghost footprint of a prehistoric lake bed that stretches all the way to the Rockies.

This is the Prairies, a geographical region 1500 kilometres wide, a place where the sky is enormous and the wind incessant. A place where, in the words of the great Prairie novelist W.O. Mitchell, you can always hear "the

> **"We spent 18 months begging people to pay attention. But by the time we hit Toronto, it went from no attention to too much attention."**

hum and twang of wind in the great prairie harp of telephone wires." Almost every day the prevailing wind would be blowing from the northwest, right into Rick's face, robbing his body of heat and pushing against him with intransigent hostility. Wind is such a fearsome enemy for athletes that wheelchair marathoners jockey for "drafting" positions—using the racer right in front of them as a windbreak.

So wheeling on the Prairies was hard, and cold, and tiring, as he knew it would be. But the terrain was flat, the highway wide and straight with good paved shoulders, and the momentum rising. They had raised $5 million and the number was still climbing.

Public response too was pushing Rick on. Along the frigid, windswept highway leading into Winnipeg, people lined up for hours, clutching $10 and $20 bills in padded mittens, waiting for the blipping police lights, and the runners, and the cyclists, and the indomitable figure in the wheelchair. As the cavalcade approached, a tremor of excitement and cheering swept through the crowd: He's coming! That's him, the Man In Motion!

In Winnipeg, Rick did 18 media interviews in one day, a new record for the Tour, and in Regina, news reporters took it upon themselves to examine and rate public buildings and facilities in their own community for wheelchair accessibility. Wherever Rick went now, it seemed that city public works departments were building curb cuts, wheelchair ramps, and accessible bathrooms. People with disabilities had always been there, but Rick's awareness campaign was bringing that community to the forefront, inspiring civic decision-makers and spurring them to action.

Dave Doroghy, as always, was staying several days ahead of the caravan, "ping ponging back and forth between restaurants," as he puts it, and only occasionally making contact with Rick and the road crew. When Rick rolled into one of the many McDonald's restaurants along the route, a fundraising campaign and celebration would already be in place.

"If something worked well in one market, we just rolled it out in another," Doroghy says. "By the time we reached Alberta, most individual McDonald's stores were raising over $10,000 each. Some of the high-volume stores were raising as much as $30,000 each."

Sometimes Doroghy cycled alongside Rick, and was often joined by other cyclists, joggers, and supporters in wheelchairs. "You had to be out there on the highway to really get a sense of what he was enduring," says Doroghy. "In temperatures that sometimes went below minus 30, Rick was out there, day in, day out, wheeling straight into a harsh wind. But that created magic. I believe the adversity he faced in western Canada, the harsh weather and unforgiving landscapes, only made Canadians love him more and back him with stronger resolve. It was a spine-tingling phenomenon. It was like the whole country was rising to its feet to applaud."

Dr. Jack Taunton, the veteran Vancouver sports medicine specialist who had treated both Terry Fox and Rick, met Rick and the road crew as they crossed the prairie. "It was incredibly cold when I joined them in Alberta," says Taunton. "My plan was to run alongside him, which I did, but I also took on the task of going out ahead of the road crew and identifying interesting people for Rick to meet. This one family I will never forget. They had a daughter with an old wooden wheelchair, and she was waiting by the highway with a poem she had written for Rick. He stopped to talk to her. He'd always been a good speaker, but he was becoming great, and it was really inspiring for me to see how the journey was transforming everyone involved, including Rick."

Canada's indigenous communities seemed particularly sympathetic to Rick's mission. Perhaps the image of a young man struggling with disadvantage resonated deeply with them. Taunton says, "I was running alongside Rick when I saw the most amazing sight. I looked up on a hill and, through a gap in the blowing snow, I saw these four First Nations elders on horseback, with spears and feathered headdresses. They had come to honour the journey of a fellow warrior. It was an extraordinary experience, and I think we all felt the power of their blessing."

That night, hundreds of people gathered in Okotoks to greet Rick. Among them were the little girl in the wooden wheelchair, and those same four elders,

125

who presented him with a sacred eagle feather. "I felt very lucky to be part of that journey," says Taunton. "I felt lucky to be part of Rick's support team. To me, he was a like a great boxer. He was getting beaten up, but we were in his corner. We would ice him down and massage his arms, make sure he was ready to go back in the ring."

As part of his message to the public, Rick was always emphasizing that he was just an average guy, and that any average person could accomplish extraordinary things if they put their mind to it. But Taunton points out that strengthening the mind is in fact the hardest challenge of all.

"I've worked with a lot of outstanding athletes," he says. "And I've learned that it actually takes a combination of attributes to make a champion. You need to have a strong vascular system, strong muscles and tendons. But most of all you need passion. Marathoners in particular need to have that fire, that determination to keep driving through the pain. People don't realize that marathons are all about pain, and Rick was doing more than two marathons every day. After working with him for years, I can say that he's one of the greatest athletes this country has ever produced, and it's largely because of his attitude."

At the border of Alberta and British Columbia, Rick was greeted by a large crowd, a mob of media, and many old friends and supporters—including Chunky Woodward, Fin Anthony, his dad, mother, and brother Brad, sister Christine, and Premier Bill Vander Zalm, who offered a cash donation matching all the funds raised on the last leg of the Tour all through BC. That donation would add up to an incredible $5.45 million. Best of all, Rick was welcomed by his mother, whose tearful hug summoned up all the emotion that Rick had worked so hard to contain for two years. "When I hugged my mom, I knew I was really coming home," he says. "It was a moment I'll never forget."

He and the road crew were facing some of the toughest mountain grades on the Tour. But they were back in their home province, and every day was

126

taking them through familiar towns and communities close to their hearts. Lee Gibson and Tim Frick also rejoined the Tour, and their presence heightened the sense of team reunification. The excitement was building.

Rick's old schoolteacher Harvey Glanville was the local coordinator for the Man In Motion Tour in Williams Lake. Rick's plan was to spend three days there, and Glanville says the entire school district had decided to take the unprecedented move of cancelling school and holding a special Rick Hansen Day. "The school district is 250 miles wide by 120 miles high [about 400 km by 195 km]," he explains. "It's a huge school district, running from Horsefly to Anahim Lake, but we organized to have every single student there. Forty yellow school buses converged on Williams Lake that Friday afternoon. It was a very emotional day. Williams Lake was vibrating!"

Glanville says the school overlooks a big field, and once the students were seated they got a wave going. "Rick came in and did a symbolic revolution of the track, passing a banner for each of the 40 schools," he says. "A First Nations boy from the reserve gave him an eagle feather and told him, 'You soar like an eagle.' Rick spoke, and the kids were just spellbound. The community too was transformed by his visit. Not only did it elevate everyone's notion of what was possible in their own lives, but we managed to raise $220,000 for the cause."

Glanville says something about Rick just fascinates kids. "My son Brook was 6 years old when the Tour was ending. He was barely old enough to understand what the Tour was about, but he was still obsessed with Rick. The Christmas after the Tour ended, I asked Brook what he wanted for a gift, and he said he wanted to go somewhere and meet Rick Hansen."

Kelly Call was too young to have met Rick when he lived in Williams Lake, but she said Rick's old teacher Bob Redford taught her phys ed. "Mr. Redford knew I was a big fan so he asked me to be the student rep on the homecoming committee. I was at the stampede grounds when Rick arrived, and I got to meet him. He was so kind and easy to talk to, really down to earth. He

> **"As part of his message to the public, Rick was always emphasizing that he was just an average guy, and that any average person could accomplish extraordinary things if they put their mind to it."**

was always thanking people, showing them how grateful he was for their support." She compiled eight scrapbooks from the Man In Motion Tour and eventually gave them all to Rick's family. "Working on the Tour was definitely one of the high points of my teenage years," she says. "It made me more idealistic and showed me what was possible."

Rick says the visit to Williams Lake was one of the best parts of the entire Tour. "My dad was a member of the organizing committee, and I was so proud that he and the rest of my family worked so hard to make that visit such a success. Ball coach and committee member Jack Burgar created a special Williams Lake McDonald's pin, which helped the community raise more money per capita than anywhere else in the country. That's a feat that I am still really grateful for today." The pin became a national best-seller that raised funds and awareness.

The last few weeks of the Tour went by in a whirl: it was an accelerating program of public appearances, small-town celebrations, and roadside crowds cheering him on. In Kamloops, he was interviewed by *People* magazine. In Nelson, a helicopter zoomed in and dumped a load of spring blossoms on the road ahead of him. In Kelowna, he passed the 24,901-mile (40,075-km) mark—the circumference of the world. It had meant an extra 400 kilometers (249 miles), to compensate for the cycle computer's calculations, which were accurate only to one one-hundredth of a kilometer. Vancouver was still a few days away, but he had done it! He had circled the world! "I can't speak for Rick," says his friend and former coach Tim Frick, "but the experience of completing that dream must have been just indescribable."

Tim rejoined the Tour just before Rick completed the circumference, and he says, "Some people gave their hard-earned money. Some gave weeks of their lives; some gave years. The Tour was made up of thousands of small and large contributions. Everyone gave more than they thought they could, thanks to Rick, whose tremendous character brought out the best in all of us."

Rick explains, "It took me a long time to get over the pain and emotional trauma of breaking my back at such a young age. I struggled with anger and self-pity, until I began to focus on the things I could do rather than the things I couldn't do. The Man In Motion Tour was my own proof that there is no limit to what anyone can accomplish if they are willing to try."

In the final days of the home stretch, it seemed almost as if Nature herself was blessing the ideals of the Tour. The dark and sullen clouds typical of the mountain passes at that time of the year seemed to lift in welcome. Great chords of sunlight leaned down through the ragged clouds and accompanied Rick as he coasted down the long precipitous grade out of the snowy coastal mountains into the verdant fields of the Fraser Valley.

In Vancouver, the largest crowds in the history of the city gathered along the streets and intersections to cheer the homecoming hero. At BC Place, 50,000 people jumped to their feet and welcomed the Man In Motion with a great, thundering burst of applause as he wheeled through the stadium, saluted by the song that had become a smash-hit anthem for brave and embattled people everywhere.

The welcome-home banner read *The End Is Just the Beginning*. Rick says, "I saw that banner and I thought, 'You've got to be kidding. I just finished wheeling this thing around the world and now you're telling me it's the beginning? The beginning of what?'"

↗ Prime Minister Brian Mulroney presents Rick with a cheque for $1 million. Muriel Honey, the Tour's media relations staff, and Jim Taylor, who was writing a book about Rick, were with Rick in Ottawa and pocketed the cheque for safekeeping—but the volunteers counting the donations didn't know and went into a panic when they couldn't find the million-dollar cheque!

↘ Mike Reid joined the Tour to provide security for Rick and the crew, especially crowd control. In Canada, the numbers increased steadily as the Man In Motion made his way across the country. Here he's mobbed by fans near London, Ontario.

→ Rick, Amanda, and hockey legend Bobby Orr. Serious athletes are bonded by dedication, discipline, and a close acquaintance with pain. While wheeling up the eastern seaboard of the USA, the Tour stopped in Boston, where Rick met his childhood hero.

↓ When Rick got to Parry Sound, Bobby Orr's hometown, he donned the Number 4 hockey jersey that Orr had given him. Snow and ice coating the rims of the wheelchair made tough work for Rick— and permanently marked the jersey's sleeves.

Rick passes by a frozen waterfall along the Trans-Canada Highway south of Wawa, Ontario. Taking advantage of the mild winter temperatures and bare roads, he wheeled 100 kilometres a day, an extra 20 kilometres over his usual daily distance.

↑ Rick and the crew spent their second Christmas on the road in Wawa. There they received a piggy bank full of coins from a local 7-year-old.

← Rick's visit to the Terry Fox Memorial near Thunder Bay was very emotional for Rick and his crew. The monument commemorates the place where Terry had to stop his Marathon of Hope because his cancer had returned.

↑ The bitter Canadian winter hit in Marathon, Ontario, where temperatures dipped to −57°C. Near Dryden, Rick fought his way through blowing snow. Scientists at Simon Fraser University had designed a winter suit equipped with sensors to monitor Rick's body temperature. It was field-tested by Vancouver wheelchair athletes Lenny Marriott and Chris Samis (who later wore shirts saying "I Was a Guinea Pig for Rick Hansen") and proved to be very effective in these cold and blustery conditions.

→ Rick with his trusty Ontario Provincial Police escorts near Dryden, Ontario. In appreciation, Rick wore a cap with the patch of each law enforcement agency that joined the team.

← Mike Pomponi joined the road crew as the winter mechanic to help Don adjust the wheelchair for optimal performance in the changing conditions. Pete Turnau and Jerry Smith had designed a 4-wheel-drive winter chair with BMX tires and specially designed chains that could be added in icy conditions. Rick rarely had to use the winter wheelchair, but it gave the crew confidence to know they had it.

↙ Whenever the weather got really difficult, someone would appear at Rick's side, keeping him company and lifting his spirits.

← After crossing the immensity of Ontario, Rick and the crew finally arrive on the prairies.

↓ All of Winnipeg seemed to have turned out to greet the Man In Motion.

→ Edie Ehlers celebrating
National Access Awareness Week
with two young supporters.

← Ten years after the
completion of the Tour,
Rick returned to China to
express his gratitude for
the overwhelming support
he'd received there. Here
he poses with Deng Pufang,
chairman of the Chinese
Welfare Fund for the Dis-
abled and son of Deng
Xiaoping, leader of the
Communist Party. After suf-
fering a spinal injury, Deng
Pufang received treatment
in Canada and joked that
he had "quite a few pints of
Canadian blood in him."

↑ Rick pondering a new beginning in the days after the Tour was over.

← The University of British Columbia invited Rick to act as a consultant for Disability Issues at the university. Rick's first priority was the establishment of the Disability Resource Centre on campus. At the opening in 1989 are UBC president David Strangway (left), Rick, and Jim King from the Ford Motor Company.

barriers in their own schools and bringing schoolmates with different abilities into group activities.

"I meet so many kids with tremendous courage and resilience who prove themselves to be great role models to their classmates," says Rick. "I'm privileged to know Emily, for example, a gifted young athlete who suffered a spinal cord injury. Thanks to enlightened and supportive teachers, she was encouraged to develop her skills as a manager of the basketball and volleyball teams, and she's made a tremendous contribution, both to the teams and to overall school spirit. She's currently training as a competitive swimmer and Paralympic hopeful for the 2020 Summer Paralympic games in Tokyo.

"Emily is now one of roughly 100 Rick Hansen Foundation Ambassadors, people with disabilities across the country who share their story at public and private events to raise awareness and inspire others in their communities. There are hundreds of kids like her, and each one has shown they have much to contribute if given the opportunity.

"Instead of one Man In Motion, it's now many in motion," says Rick. "Young people are the pioneers of the future. And it's really important for them to learn from our mistakes and our successes, and to be inspired to take action. There are over 1.1 billion people with disabilities in the world (approximately 15 percent), and that number will keep rising with population growth and the aging of the baby boomers. So we are not just a small special interest group. People with disabilities are the world's largest minority."

154

People with disabilities have made encouraging progress since the completion of the Man In Motion Tour. And as accessibility and inclusivity have improved, society has benefited in countless ways. But the journey is still underway, and young people will be its champions. "Let's keep the wheels turning," says Rick. "The best is still to come."

dollars of research grants, and also helped to establish five leadership endowments worth $20 million.

In 2008, the Blusson Spinal Cord Centre was built to house ICORD, the Rick Hansen Institute (RHI), and other multidisciplinary leaders in the field so that they can work together under one roof towards their common goal of promoting full functional recovery and improved quality of life for people living with SCI.

RHI was created to develop a global network of collaborators that work together to validate the most promising discoveries, and accelerate progress to improve health outcomes and cures for paralysis after SCI.

Rick and the foundation have also launched numerous other programs that are not easily quantified in dollar terms but that have heightened awareness in the general public and changed the dialogue on the issues of people with disability.

The Rick Hansen School Program, for example, teaches students about the potential of people with disabilities and empowers students to make a positive difference in their schools and communities. Bilingual educational modules are available to all schools in Canada for free, and each year, thousands of schools deliver the program to over half a million students. As Rick puts it, "The Rick Hansen School Program aspires to get the support of every young person in the country. There's a long journey still ahead and we need their help to get there."

The value of the Rick Hansen School Program is in removing the apparent differences between students with disabilities and their schoolmates. Students who go through the program learn about the determination and courage of the kids with disabilities they see every day in their school's hallways and classrooms. They hear their stories—perhaps for the first time—and come to realize that those kids actually might be as "cool" as they are. Teachers who have implemented the program say their students show greater empathy for people with disabilities and a much greater interest in removing

"The banner that greeted Rick when he returned home to Vancouver ('The End Is Just the Beginning') was turning out to be dead on."

———

an accessibility advisor to the university, allowing Rick to concentrate on the work that was becoming a lifetime passion. He says, "Rick was hired as the National Fellow and was a driving force in the creation of the Disability Resource Centre, an office that welcomes and improves access for disabled students, faculty, staff, and visitors. The centre coordinates services such as mobility assistance, specialized exam assistance, captioning, and interpreting."

The banner that greeted Rick when he returned home to Vancouver ("The End Is Just the Beginning") was turning out to be dead on. Soon the Rick Hansen Foundation partnered with UBC, and Rick's "short-term" job with the university turned into a 15-year commitment. They were back on the road again! Rick's tenure at UBC brought sweeping and fundamental changes to the campus. Says Strangway, "Many of our buildings were old and required retrofitting. That was a good lesson because retrofitting is much more expensive than making buildings accessible in the first place." Rick's friend Sue Paish says his campaign to make UBC accessible was daunting and complicated. "It seemed to require about 15 pages of permits for every improvement to the campus infrastructure. And even the most minor initiatives were tangled in red tape. At times he got very frustrated. But as we all know, barriers can't stop Rick. When you're walking at UBC and you see a power door or a curb cut, that's Rick Hansen."

Rick's term at UBC generated more than improvements for accessibility. Rick and the Foundation realized that if gains were to be made in progress towards finding cures for paralysis after SCI, the fragmented community needed to be connected and unified.

They helped create world-class research leadership capacity at UBC by supporting the development of the research centre International Collaboration on Repair Discoveries (ICORD), led by Dr. John Steeves, through millions of

152

Long-serving board member Russ Anthony says, "We were like the dog that caught the bus. First our problem was having no money. Then the problem was having millions that needed to be managed wisely. We felt a real moral obligation to make sure that our many donors would support whatever way we ended up using the money. We looked at different options. Rick could have travelled the world and spent a lifetime commercializing himself."

As the revenues were tallied up against expenses, Rick and the team were thrilled to calculate that the Tour had cost $1.7 million and generated $26 million. (Since then, a remarkable $342 million has been raised.) Everyone felt it was important to spread some of the revenue to the charitable groups that had supported the cause, so $2.6 million went to Alberta and another $2 million was distributed to organizations across the rest of Canada. Twenty million was used to create the Rick Hansen Man In Motion Legacy Fund, and the interest generated was distributed annually in the form of grants to worthwhile charities and projects in support of spinal cord injury (SCI) research, rehabilitation, and wheelchair sport.

As Rick considered his future options, federal minister of international trade Pat Carney asked him to represent Canada in Australia at Expo 88. So after Rick and Amanda got married in October of 1987, they moved to Brisbane, where he became the Commissioner-General of the Canadian Pavilion for the duration of Expo 88. During that time, he made the commitment to stay involved with the work he'd started with the Man In Motion Tour.

When he returned from Australia, Rick immediately teamed up with the Man In Motion board to launch the Rick Hansen Foundation (RHF)—a charitable foundation committed to promoting awareness, supporting quality of life and removing barriers for people with disabilities, and inspiring an inclusive society.

That same year, the president of the University of British Columbia, David Strangway, reached out to Rick because he had "ignited the issue of accessibility globally, and in so doing had put the onus on us, right here at home, to make our campus more inclusive." Strangway offered Rick a full-time job as hotel I was clear in my head. I was done with the Tour and ready to start my security company."

At Man In Motion headquarters, the printers were quiet and Edie Ehlers was cleaning up. The place had the abandoned feeling of an apartment after a New Year's Eve party. "The end of the tour was a real anticlimax," she says. "I didn't even get to see the Tour come by our office building, but I did get to Oakridge for the welcome-home ceremonies because someone had to stay in the office and look after the thousands of donations coming in the door."

The young advertising man Dave Doroghy was similarly at a loss. "Being on the road with the Man In Motion Tour was the most exciting thing I had ever done. And I had the feeling that I would never do anything so important again. I was Wile E. Coyote after he's run off a cliff."

Rick says he realized he was still young, strong, and vigorous, and he didn't want to rest on his laurels. "The end of the Tour made it clear that I had to take a new path. I wasn't much interested in competition anymore, even though I was at my peak athletically. The Tour had transformed my aspirations, broadened my path. I wanted to do more than compete as an athlete."

"Rick is a very respectful guy, and it had to be something he would feel good about," says McDonald's Canada president George Cohon. "When he got back to Vancouver I took him aside and said, 'You need to do some kind of commemorative event yearly.' But he said he didn't want to do anything that might distract from the annual Terry Fox Run."

Bill McIntosh of Nike was still on the Man In Motion board of directors and says Rick and the board members had a big question in front of them: What to do with the money they'd raised? "We were looking at two options," says McIntosh. "We could just give it all away to deserving charities or create a foundation and put the interest towards rehab, wheelchair sports, and a cure. People would apply and we would dole out grants from the interest money every year. But maybe Rick wanted to do something else? I think it was a hard choice for him."

← "The Tour transformed everyone who was involved with it," says Rick. "By working together for a common goal, we suffered together, supported each other, and became better versions of ourselves."

THE LEGACY

———

I can see a new horizon underneath the blazin' sky
I'll be where the eagle's flying higher and higher.
—"ST. ELMO'S FIRE"

EVERYONE KNEW THAT THE daily grind of the Tour would test their endurance and character, but the deafening silence that came afterwards was a test that caught them off guard.

The crew had no money, no place to live, no game plan. Getting down the road was their plan, but they had run out of road. Some of them checked into the Sheraton Hotel in downtown Vancouver. "You have to remember that we had pretty much given up our own budding careers and whatever personal relationships to devote ourselves to the Tour," says Mike Reid, "so there was a real feeling of loss. I don't know about everyone else, but I had never felt lost before. I sat in my empty hotel room, looking out the window thinking, 'Now what?'"

After a few days of rest and contemplation, he laced up his sneakers and went for a long hike. "I walked through Kitsilano all the way to Jericho Beach and back. It was a two-and-a-half-hour walk, and by the time I got back to the

149

THE END IS JUST THE BEGINNING
Welcome Home Rick

MILES (40,000 KM.)

10

↑ The Man In Motion World Tour team. From left to right: Mike Pomponi, Don Alder, Mike Reid, Simon Cumming, Derek Hill, Nancy Thompson, Amanda Hansen, and Rick Hansen.

← Vancouver spelled out its thanks.

→ Supporters even sought out nearby roofs to catch a glimpse of the Man In Motion.

↓ Ron Marcoux, Western Vice President, presenting a final cheque on behalf of McDonald's Canada.

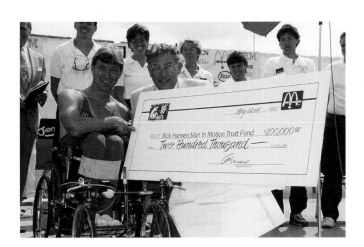

→ The following day, Rick is welcomed home by a crowd of 50,000 people at a free public celebration at BC Place Stadium in Vancouver. He receives a standing ovation. The event is televised nationally and the *Vancouver Sun* issues a special edition devoted to the Tour.

↑ At Canada Place in Vancouver, a giant thermometer measured the Tour's progress towards its goal of raising $10 million. Here board members Marshal Smith (left) and Doug Mowat celebrate reaching that milestone.

↖ Rick meets with enthusiastic Brownies in Princeton, BC. With just over a week to go before the end of the Tour, everyone was curious to meet the man who had just set a Guinness World Record for the longest wheelchair marathon.

← On May 22, 1987, Rick rolls into the Oakridge Centre in Vancouver, where the Man In Motion Tour began more than 40,000 kilometres earlier. Thousands of people lined the streets to cheer him on, waving yellow plastic ribbons printed with "Welcome Home Rick."

← Williams Lake offered Rick a hero's homecoming. Schools were closed for the day, and friends and family came out to show their support. Back row (left to right): Granny Elsie Gibson; Rick's father, Marvin Hansen; Grandma Hilderberg; brother-in-law Geordie Moore; sisters Cindy and Christine. Front row: Rick and his mother, Joan Hansen.

↑ Rick doing a lap of the track at Williams Lake Junior high school, his alma mater, to roaring crowds.

← Rick fishing with his brother Brad during a rest day in Valemount.

↓ In the winter months, Rick and the crew were usually on the road before the sun came up.

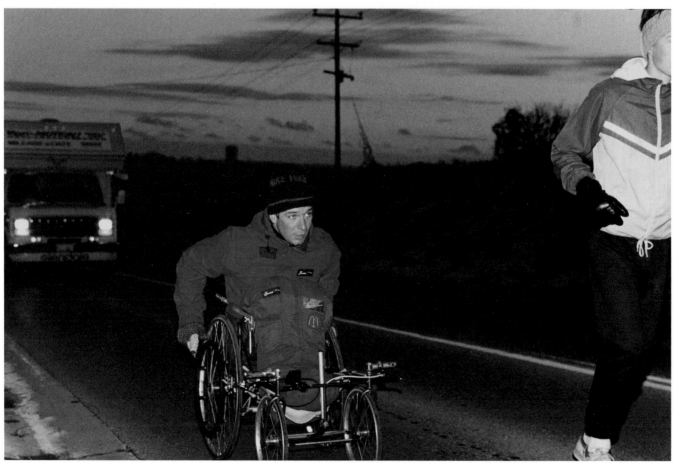

← Rick stops at the viewpoint for Mount Terry Fox, which lies off Highway 16 about 3 hours east of Prince George, close to Mt. Robson's west gate.

↑ As Rick crossed over into British Columbia, he found himself in familiar terrain and the donations kept pouring in. The Tour would raise nearly $15 million in BC alone in just 2 months.

↑ As the Tour hit Kelowna, BC, Rick was happy about the great weather and friendly crowds, May 7, 1987.

↑ Rick and the crew felt great excitement as they reached their last provincial border, from Alberta back into British Columbia. From left to right: Simon Cumming, Lee Gibson, Don Alder, Nancy Thompson, Amanda Reid, Mike Reid, Mike Pomponi, Rico Bond, and Derrick Hill. Rick led the way.

← Homeward bound. Rick is greeted by his mother, Joan Hansen, at the BC border.

Rick Hansen "Man in Motion" commemorative plate by Wedgwood

Wedgwood salutes the courageous efforts of Rick Hansen's "Man in Motion" World Tour to raise awareness and funds for Spinal Cord Research and Rehabilitation.

In honour of this outstanding accomplishment, Wedgwood has created this commemorative plate in a limited edition of 2,500.

Available at:

6.5" Blue Jasper in a Limited Edition

$00.00

$5.00 will be donated to the Rick Hansen Fund for Spinal Cord Research and Rehabilitation for every plate sold.

DEALER NAME & ADDRESS

Wedgwood®

↑ Wedgewood issued a limited-edition (2,500) commemorative plate in its signature blue Jasperware china to help raise funds for the Tour and spinal cord research. Many companies and individuals offered sponsorship with in-kind donations, branded products, and innovative marketing campaigns.

↖ Fundraisers in Alberta asked individuals and groups to donate to the Tour by "purchasing" a kilometre of the "Hansen Highway," each marked with a post. Wayne Gretzky sponsored Kilometre 99, of course.

← Tour merchandise manager Derrick Hill with just some of the buttons, badges, and pennants issued to support the Tour.

→ McDonald's Restaurants had been raising money for the Tour all the way across the country. By the time Rick and the crew reached Regina, they were regularly receiving large cheques from franchises. The company also provided Rick and the crew with complimentary meals all around the world.

↓ Children are particularly fascinated by Rick and his adventuring spirit. One 6-year-old boy in Williams Lake told his father, "All I want for Christmas is to meet Rick Hansen."

↑ A sure-fire indicator of having arrived in the west: cowboy hats. Rick rolled into Saskatchewan and declared, "Only two more borders to go!" After nearly 2 years on the road, the momentum was rising as the Tour headed steadily towards Vancouver.

→ In addition to cyclists and runners, horse riders accompanied Rick across Saskatchewan.

↑ Rick dropped the puck at a few National Hockey League games, including this match-up between the Edmonton Oilers and the Winnipeg Jets. Wayne Gretzky faces off against Dale Hawerchuk.

← In Winnipeg, Rick gave 18 media interviews in a single day, the most of any city on the entire Tour.

↑ In 2002, the Rick Hansen Institute organized the first Wheels in Motion fundraising event, in Toronto. Today, communities across Canada run wheelchair obstacle courses, timed races, and wheels/walks to raise money in support of spinal cord injury research and rehabilitation.

← Rick with Premier Gordon Campbell (centre) and Prime Minister Stephen Harper (right) at the Blusson Spinal Cord Centre in Vancouver in 2010.

→ Rick addressing the crowd at the Opening Ceremonies of the 2010 Paralympic Winter Games.

←↓ Rick was one of the five final torchbearers during the 2010 Winter Olympic and Paralympic Games in Vancouver. Here, he enters BC Place Stadium to kick off the Opening Ceremonies.

→ To celebrate the 25th Anniversary of the Man In Motion Tour, Rick returned to the Great Wall of China with hundreds of international students in April 2011.

↓ In Canada, Rick celebrated the 25th Anniversary with a relay across the country, retracing the route of the original Tour. With Tyrone Henry (in the wheelchair to the left of Rick, in dark navy blue outfit) and other relay participants, in May 2011 he wheeled up Coquitlam's Thermal Hill Drive, a 17.5% grade and the steepest of the entire Tour.

← Rick and George Cohon on May 22, 2012, in Vancouver on the last day of the 25th Anniversary Relay.

↓ Rick and the Foundation team in 2015, symbolizing a more connected world with many in motion.

A WORLD WITHOUT BARRIERS